when we were miners

D1575138

when we were miners

ian isaac

NUM (South Wales Area)
BALLOT FOR AREA PRESIDENT

VOTE FOR
IAN ISAAC
A MINERS' PRESIDENT
ON A MINER'S WAGE

Published by Ken Smith Press

When We Were Miners
Ian Isaac

© Ian Isaac, 2010
Published by Ken Smith Press, 2010
First Edition March 2010

ISBN 978-0-9564720-0-7 pbk

Typeset in Utopia 9 pt
Printed by Gwasg Dinefwr Press, Carmarthenshire
Cover Design: Owain Isaac

typesetting & page layout: dennis@kavitagraphics.co.uk

Acknowledgements

The final appearance of this account would not have been possible without the editing skills of Ken Smith, who has himself written a book about the 1984/5 Miners' Strike. It is called: The Miners Strike a civil war without guns. Ken has been a friend for more than 25 years, and as well as having played a direct part in this account between March and November 1984, he proved able to stand outside the events and offer impartial advice and encouragement when I felt unable to master the extended art of writing a book. I write email notes, instructions, memorandums, reports and papers every day for a living, but this project was something different. I had to dig deep to get the balance right.

My thanks to Peter Skelly, a national officer of the RMT union, whose acquaintance I had renewed after 25 years, and he was kind enough to provide early feedback and corrections to first drafts of this account that proved helpful in establishing the discipline of being factually correct as far as can be achieved.

My appreciation goes to Christine Esposito for her help and advice in the reading, spelling and style corrections in the first and final drafts and to Natalie Wearne for copy typing sections from my archives. My father Idwal, at 86 years of age, offered some timely advice in the first parts of my account and of course had a part to play in the account itself. His quest to publish his own short autobiographical stories became as important to me as publishing this account.

To my partner, Margaret, for understanding my endeavour - even though it must seem like another world and another time to her. Her own recollections of her father Harry Davies waiting in line at Swansea docks for casual work are closer to my experience than to hers, for she was so young at the time.

Also, my appreciation to my son Owain, who lived through these events as a boy and a teenager, from the ages of three to 18, and who gave the final touches with his superb illustrations for the book and feedback from readings of various drafts. His daughter Xena (aged thirteen) making her own inquiries.

My daughter Emma, who was aged three to eight during the strike and subsequent struggles read through the drafts and provided some feedback. Her young children Ffion (aged nine) and Carys (aged six) were fascinated by some of the pictures.

Dedication

To the memory of Andrew Glyn (1944-2008) an Oxford economist and author with an art for simple explanation of complex matters who was a collaborator and friend of the miners and working people. Our time discussing and working together will remain in my memory.

Foreword
by Phil White and Ken Smith

THE publication of Ian Isaac's book, When We Were Miners, to mark the 25th anniversary of the ending of the 1984-85 miners' strike, is timely. Most people who follow modern history know, in broad terms, what the strike was about, and how it led to the defeat of the NUM, which set in train a process of further attacks on working people and their trade unions, the subsequent demise of the pits in Britain, and the devastation of working class-communities that often followed in its wake.

Some of the biggest lies ever perpetrated in history were used to justify the destruction of the mining industry in Britain, and the official accounts of those events do nothing to challenge that perception. As Ian remarks in the book, it is a case of "to the victor the spoils".

Yet, for many, looking back at the events of the 1980s and 1990s in the coal industry there is an increasing questioning of the official events and the lies and myths perpetrated about it - particularly what could be regarded as the two big lies.

The first was that in the run-up to and during the 1984-85 miners' strike many of the pits in the British coalfields were uneconomic and had to be shut accordingly to stop "losing" money for the taxpayer. The second big lie has been that it was the miners' decision to take strike action in 1984-85 that led to the speeded-up demise of the industry.

Neither is true. The run-down of the mining industry in Britain and the attack on the National Union of Mineworkers were both "essential" components of a counter-revolution carried out in Britain by Margaret Thatcher's Tory government to implement a neo-liberal economic agenda - a brutal combination of letting the free market rip and attacks on working-class living standards and conditions - a strategy which is having disastrous consequences for the majority of people in Britain to this day. And, it is proving equally disastrous for the long-term provision of energy in Britain.

The closure of the coal mines had ruinous results in the mining communities of Britain and beyond. As Ian outlines in the book, the neo-liberal programme of Thatcherism and big business - continued by New Labour when in power - is still wreaking havoc in the lives of ordinary people through the economic meltdown of 2008 and the continuing recession.

Ian's book, although primarily a personal account of his role in the South Wales coalfield and NUM from 1974 to 1991, demolishes those lies and shows that there could have been a better outcome that would have greatly improved the lives of the majority of people living in the UK.

The book gives a full and unique flavour of the battles over the future of coal in the South Wales area, while also setting it in the context of the wider national and international political developments of the time. This book will be seen by present and future generations as a useful guide to what the real debate was. We believe it will go some way to rectify the ideological imbalance there has been in coverage of the miners' cause and help give a clearer picture of what really happened on the ground.

Both of us were participants - to one degree or another - in the events outlined in this book, and of course that common struggle has created a strong bond of friendship and comradeship that lasts to this day.

You cannot experience such a living struggle and work so closely with people during an event like the 1984-85 strike without it staying with you for the rest of your life. Such a bond is not borne, however, out of sentimentality or romance for the strike or its aftermath.

1984 was the year of the dystopian nightmare of George Orwell's book. It was a year of Frankie's Two Tribes and it was a year where the state turned on its people. But most of all it was a year of battle between two ways of life and looking at society.

One view was that of Gordon Gecko's in the film Wall Street that "Greed is good" and the other was a society of solidarity and common decency trying to improve the position of working-class people.

The perception is that it was the first view that won. But that is not quite true. The fact that the miners fought in 1984-85, and beyond, backed up by the support of millions in Britain and internationally, left a lasting imprint that showed itself most visibly in the mass uprising against the Tory Government's proposed pit closure programme in 1992 and the poll tax riots which resulted in a complete U-turn by the Tory government of John Major in 1992.

And that imprint lasts to this day, with more and more questioning the politics of neo-liberalism or Thatcherism. Only a few years ago the proposal by Gordon Brown's government to give Baroness Thatcher a state funeral provoked outrage, such is the bitterness of the legacy her term in office and policies have left.

All of us struggled for a different outcome that we believed could save the mining industry and communities that were being destroyed at the altar of Thatcherism. Again, that was not for sentimental reasons, there are still 300 years of coal reserves in Britain that could be extracted in an environmentally friendly way, and that could be used to provide jobs, cheaper fuel and a sense of community that would greatly enrich the lives of working-class people in this country.

And it was also to preserve the positive values that had been brought about by trade union struggle in the mining industry and communities. We were acutely aware at the time that the defeat of the miners in 1984-85 would lead to a more divided society with increased social and economic problems and a breakdown of communities in some areas.

Many accounts try to portray the defeat of the miners' strike as the Year Zero for the end of trade unionism. But, as Ian shows, there were battles still going on to save the pits and also to stop the NUM and unions from moving to the right and acquiescing in the Tory attacks on working-class people.

That was at the heart of Ian's efforts, along with others to build a Broad Left in the NUM and support Arthur Scargill's re-election campaign. Contrary to the impression given in some quarters, it was not about individuals gaining positions within the union movement, it was about the direction and future of the movement.

There was a battle going on for the heart of the NUM's soul, where a young and fresh leadership was emerging putting forward a socialist programme for the NUM and the energy industry.

Ian was at the head of a group of younger miners' leaders who became battle-hardened by the events of the strike. Had the strike been victorious then there is no doubt that Ian and other miners would have formed new area and national leaderships of the NUM after the strike. The nucleus of this new leadership would have included miners like the late Joe Owens from Scotland, who died tragically young at the age of 45 at the end of 2009, and Chris Herriot also from Scotland. Also among their ranks would have been Tyrone O'Sullivan and Phil White from Wales, John Cunningham and Stan Pearce from Northumberland and Durham and many others, such as Gary Ironmonger and Richard Clarkson in Yorkshire.

Despite that defeat, it was the efforts of Ian and others, in campaigns like that of the St John's miners to save their pit and retain a fighting leadership for their trade union that ensured that unions are still very much around today. They say if you live long enough then nothing surprises you anymore. Well, although still relative youngsters at heart, we find it incredible to see, just 25 years after we were told there were no government subsidies available to keep the pits open, the breathtaking sums being flooded into the City of London and international banking institutions to prop up a failed, diseased and corrupt industrial sector.

Some estimates calculate this "quantative easing" has cost £1.6 trillion - the equivalent of 18 months UK Government spending.

If just a fraction of that money had been used - under one-sixtieth, or less than £30 billion - over the past 25 years, then a highly efficient, green and socially useful energy industry based on coal could have been developed, which would have preserved expertise and tens of thousands of jobs that have been lost forever.

Now, although some private firms such as Tata are looking to open private deep coal mines in South Wales to provide "economic" coal for their steelworks at Port Talbot, it is unlikely that coal mining will ever exist again in South Wales on the mass scale it once did.

If only there had been that level of investment in coal, then we would not be embarking on a nuclear build programme of new power stations. As was always stated during the strike, "coal was for the future", particularly if it was combined with clean coal technology. Britain and its poorest communities (most of which are in traditional mining areas today) would not now find themselves at the mercy of the multinational utility companies, and the ever-increasing cost of energy being delivered to our homes. Coal would have been available to generate electricity and heat to all, and it would be a far more affordable energy than what is available to most of the poorest communities in Britain today

But coal mining in South Wales - as in other areas - was more than just a big industry; it was a way of life. And the great service Ian Isaac has done in writing this book is to recapture that way of life - warts and all - to show future generations what life was like When We Were Miners.

Phil White and **Ken Smith**, *March 2010*

Part one:
1974 to 1984:
Ten years preparing for battle

1 The long view

I N 1972, Lord Robens, one-time chairman of the NCB wrote a book, Ten-Year Stint. From his time as chairman of the NCB (1961 to 1971), he gained two reputations: One for whitewashing the inquiry about the terrible tragedy of Aberfan (October 21, 1966), when 116 schoolchildren and 28 adults lost their lives when an avalanche of small coal slurry slid down a mountainside in the Taff valley engulfing the school and all within it.

This was in the days before the Health and Safety Executive had been established and there was no conception of the phrase "corporate manslaughter". Who knows if guilt was to become a motivator, but in 1972 he published the Robens Report that led to the Health and Safety at Work Act 1974, which has been the template for Health and Safety practice ever since.

Robens' other reputation was for the number of collieries that he had closed under a Labour Government. Although appointed by Harold Macmillan in 1961, at the tail end of a Tory Government that had been in power for more than 10 years, Robens a former, shopworkers union (Usdaw) official and backbench Labour MP was to retain his position as chairman of the NCB until 1971. During that time 400 collieries closed and 300,000 miners' jobs vanished. (The Independent, Obituary: Lord Robens of Woldingham, June 29, 1999)

The industry before nationalisation

P rior to nationalisation, the former coal owners, before and during the Second World War, had asset-stripped the mining industry, failed to invest in safe practices and borrowed money from banks and finance houses to pay out to shareholders and bonuses for themselves, they thereby left the British coal industry looking like a collection of 19th Century mining museums. At least it was like that in Wales, where former owners and government had done the same to the railway industry; most of mining was also connected to the railways in one way or another. The 1945 Labour Government rescued ailing underinvested private industries in rail, and mining as well as establishing the National Health Service in 1948 led by health minister Aneurin Bevan, a former Tredegar NUM lodge official in the South Wales Miners' Federation.

The railway links

Virtually every mine was linked by rail for freight, and in many cases had a station or a halt for men travelling to work. Railways linked the valleys together and encouraged trade and shopping between communities.

It was another contemporary of Alf Robens, Dr Richard Beeching, who as chairman of British Rail presided over another act of industrial butchery by breaking up the railway system, that had connected the mines to the communities, docks, factories and steel works.

In 1962, a study took place into traffic flows on the railways which concluded that 30 per cent of miles carried just one per cent of passengers and freight and half of all stations contributed to just two per cent of income.

Beeching's report, The Reshaping of British Railways, in 1963, proposed that 18,000 miles of railway, 6,000 of which was mostly rural branch lines and cross country lines, should close.

The rail closures came to a halt in the 1970s, when it became apparent that they were not useful and the small amount of money saved by closing railways was outweighed by the congestion and pollution caused by increasing reliance on cars which followed.

The public hated the cuts in railway services and the 1973 oil crisis proved the final end of large scale railway closures.

It is ironic that now in the 21st Century in the Llynfi Valley a rail service has been restored to Maesteg town centre linking it to Bridgend and Cardiff. However, the railway linking the Llynfi and Afan valleys has not been replaced.

It was the line that my grandfather Emlyn Isaac, with his overman friend Tony Mort, travelled to work on from Cwmfelin via Maesteg, Caerau, and through the tunnel to Cymmer on to Duffryn Rhondda Colliery.

Lack of investment

The NCB did little to invest in sufficient amounts to modernise the mining industry in Wales. They did introduce, 10 years later than in England, power loading instead of the old semi-conventional workings, where miners would hew the coal literally by pick and shovel from up close to the coal face which would then be shovelled onto a chain-loading system immediately behind the miners within the confines of coal seams typically less than 4ft high. A 5ft or 6ft seam, allowing miners to stand up in, was a rarity.

Power loading saw the introduction of steel ploughs which would rip into the seam at ground level thereby loading the coal onto electrically driven chain convey-ors. Colliers in the 1970s still had to set Dowty props and bars in the pits, as they had been doing for more than 50 years.

The NCB did sink a new mine in Abernant, between Neath and Ammanford, in the 1960s and drove a slant into the anthracite coal reserves at Betws near Ammanford.

By the late 1970s the props and roof bars were being replaced by walking chocks (hydraulically operated cages), that would pin themselves to the roof of the seams after moving tight to the coal seams after the plough or Doscoe (machines with huge drums with pikes laid in a helix that would gouge the coal as it travelled along biting into the coal seam).

Welsh coal faces

Coal faces would be typically 100 yards long or less in Wales. In England, coal faces more than 200 yards long were not uncommon. In England, the coal seams were as flat as the topography above them, but in Wales the seams resembled the rolling hills, mountains and valleys above the coal seams.

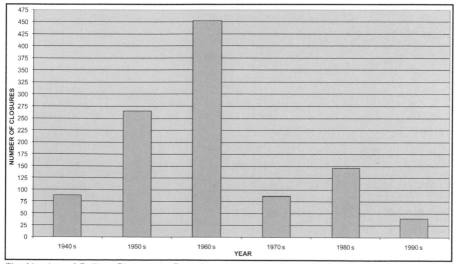

The Number of Colliery Closures by Decade

Mining coal was an acquired art in Wales compared to the factory-like conditions that prevailed in much of the Midlands and Yorkshire coalfields.

Conditions and pay had also traditionally been better in the English coalfields despite the efforts of Will Paynter, the union's national president, to standardise the wages systems through the introduction of the Power Loading Agreement (PLA) in 1966.

Over time bonus systems had crept into the mining industry, and this often led to one area being pitched against another when it came to calls for solidarity over pay issues or improvement of conditions and ultimately over the struggle to retain jobs in mining communities.

Today, 1,059,673 tonnes of coal is being produced in Wales annually from a few private small mines and opencast operations. [mainly in the county of Neath Port Talbot]. In the UK 9,446.365 tonnes were produced against a known coal reserve of 54,048 million. In 10 to 15 years we will run out of opencast coal without displacing whole populations of former mining communities.[1]

Before coal mining

The valleys had been beautiful places, full of hill farming with sheep on the mountains and arable land sustaining small populations of Welsh-speaking villages and market towns. The discovery of iron by industrial capitalist investors in the 17th and 18th Centuries helped to fuel a new iron age of industrial revolution.

Generally, where there was iron there was coal. Geologists soon discovered that where there were outcrops of limestone there would be coal seams beneath.

Limestone is a porous by-product of layers of shells of sea creatures squashed together in layers until they form a sedimentary rock emanating from the oceans millions of years ago. Coal had been laid down by forestation and vegetation over millions of years, and then squeezed like sponges over the top of the porous limestone until hardened.

The older the coal, the harder it became. Hence, the best and hardest coal in virtually the whole world is anthracite, which was found in abundance in the west of the South Wales coalfield from Duffryn Rhondda, through Hirwaun and the Neath and Swansea valleys to Pembrokeshire.

Coking coal - most used in ships' boilers and steel works - came from the middle of the coalfield from the Rhondda down to the coast through Llanharran and Llynfi, Garw and Ogmore Valleys.

A softer, though no less useful steam coal, was mined in the east of the coalfield around Torfaen, Ebbw Vale, and at the Heads of the Valleys, towards Fochriw and Oglevy and Blaeanavon. My father had worked at Oglevy Colliery and the family lived at Fochriw for a few years when I was a child.

Associations of working men and miners

Associations of working men, and eventually the trade unions and political parties representing working men, developed directly from the experience of exploitation of their labour by the owners of industry. The iron masters, having brought vast numbers of landless labourers to the coalfields in search of work faced the challenge of industrial labourers seeking to freely associate for social, cultural and religious reasons, and then later in the 18th Century embarking on the struggle to form trade unions.

It is no accident that the NUM, the successor to the South Wales Miners Federation, had a branch structure called lodges. This was the term used by various guilds and societies before and during the industrial revolution.

Craft guilds developed from being secretive religious societies, such as the mediaeval Freemasons, and later the Royal Antediluvian Order of Buffaloes (ROAB) or 'Buffs', a working man's version of the Freemasons.

These secret societies adhered to an Old Testament view of the Bible, which believed in a God that was an architect, thereby justifying the creation of wealth and private profit. So for miners to call their associations lodges, the same as the Freemasons and Buffs, was in a sense a legitimising of their quest for fairness and the right to association - particularly at times of economic hardship, an endemic state of affairs in the mining industry throughout the 18th and 19th Centuries.

The battles for recognition, the right to organise and provision of education for one's fellow workers was a struggle that took place through the trade unions well into the 20th Century. These struggles challenged head on the old master and servant relationship that still to this day underpins British common law and the law of contract. The expectation of deference by the master of the servant was breaking down in Victorian society.

The workers and miners' associations established miners' libraries and self-help education schemes via the Workers Education' Association (WEA) and National Central Labour College (NCLC). The WEA was a Trade Union Congress (TUC) sponsored educational arm, while the NCLC had a more radical reputation being sponsored by the Independent Labour Party, the Communist Party and other parties as well as individual trade unions. The TUC campaigned to bar its members from affiliating to the NCLC in the 1930s.

These bodies helped to create a more radical type of local leader, such as Aneurin Bevin in Tredegar. Bevan attended the NCLC College in London. He later went on to become MP for Tredegar and, health minister under the 1945 Attlee Labour Government. He is, of course, widely regarded for forming the NHS in Britain.

Other histories of the miners have described in detail the struggles of Arthur [AJ] Cook (who became leader of the Miners' Federation of Great Britain and led the miners during the 1926 general strike and six-month miners' strike that followed).

When Cook was elected in 1924 as general secretary of the MFGB he stated that he took it that those men who voted for him knew his policy – "that is for industrial unionism, and the carrying out of my work with regard to Marxian economics and philosophy. I will not rest satisfied until private enterprise in the mining industry is abolished. I know this can only be accomplished in stages, but I have definitely made it a goal to aim for. We can only get what we are strong enough to win and retain." This, according to Paul Davies, of the A J Cook Memorial Committee, was a watchword for young miners in the Rhondda in first two decades of the 20th Century.[2]

'Not a penny off the pay – not a second on the day' - slogan of the MFGB promoted by A J Cook

A J Cook

A pamphlet written by A J Cook himself explains the bitterness felt by the miners' representatives of more than one million miners who were prevented from taking part in the TUC general council decisions that colluded with the government of the day to end the nine-day general strike, with no guarantees that employers would reduce wages and increase hours. R H Thomas of the TUC general council was particularly singled out for criticism for not allowing the miners a say in the TUC decision to agree with Lord Samuelson and the Government call for a return to work and abandon support for the miners. So the miners battled on alone.

Cook still extolled the support shown by ordinary workers in the nine-day general strike. He thought a few days more of the general strike would have resulted in a settlement in favour of the miners and the whole of the Labour and union movement.

It was A J Cook, in mid-August 1926, after six months on strike who stated: "I have never believed that the miners could win alone".

"If you want a scapegoat, I am here to be that ... I am willing to be sacrificed... it seems to me if we sit still, it gradually becomes a position of district by district, pit by pit.... better to face this now than in a month's time... I ask you to face the position or produce some alternative, or at least prepare some other means of victory".

By November 1926, the MFGB had agreed to return to work. It was left to each pit to negotiate what were the best terms they could achieve in terms of hours and pay.

There was no prospect of a national agreement let alone a political commitment to nationalisation. (The 1984-85 miners' strike was to end in similar terms, without agreement).

Cook continued to regain what ground he could on hours and wages in the years ahead. He said: "We have lost ground, but we shall regain it in a very short time by using our industrial and political machines".

Cook, by 1926, was not quite the syndicalist that some academics have described him as. "It is not eloquence which counts in negotiations, but organised power" (A J Cook, on the eve of a Labour election victory in 1929).

Noah Ablett had warned that "we don't have to cross the river to fill the pale". Ablett was the author of The Miners' Next Step, a syndicalist pamphlet distributed widely in the South Wales Coalfield in 1912 demanding a minimum wage for miners and for control of the mines to be given to the miners. He was on the national executive committee of the Miners' Federation of Great Britain during the 1920s. Syndicalism reflected a belief that society could be changed through militant trade unionism without having to participate in a revolutionary political party.

The miners' problems were to be resolved through militant action through the miners' unions and the local institutions themselves. They fostered a belief that they didn't need support from the rest of the trade union and labour movement.

These syndicalist sentiments expressed a view that society could be changed through the concerted action of the miners and their trade union.

There was also a belief that socialism could be achieved in this way as well, and not through a political and industrial struggle throughout society itself. Later, in the 1940s and 1950s, Arthur Horner a protégé of Noah Ablett who held Marxist education classes in Ynyshir, in the Rhondda, was elected first general secretary of the unified National Union of Mineworkers (NUM) in 1946. He had been president of the South Wales Miners' Federation from 1936 to 1946. Horner was a famous Communist organiser and founder member in 1921 of the Communist Party of Great Britain

Horner had spent a lifetime in struggle, having been imprisoned for avoiding conscription in 1915, moving to Ireland and taking part in the Easter Uprising. In 1932 he was again imprisoned for unlawful assembly but was released following a hunger strike and a magnificent campaign by the SWMF.

Having read Karl Marx, Arthur Horner later described labour as a commodity. A commodity, as any first-year economics student will know, can be exchanged for money. Therefore, the role of the union leader is to ensure that the owners of industry buy their labour from the trade unions.

By the time of the war he continued to gain significant improvements in the conditions and pay of the miners. He then became a responsible for directing the NUM's strategy towards the nationalisation of the coal mines in 1947. He warned before he retired in 1958: "The Arabs won't live in tents forever", referring to the laissez faire importation of cheap oil and the sacrifice of pits on the basis of that cheap oil in the 1960s.

It was mainly British oil companies that owned and distributed the oil from Arab countries until those countries nationalised their oil industries in the 1960s which resulted in the doubling of the price of oil in 1974.

The price of oil rose from $2.50 a barrel in 1948 to $3 in 1957, and from 1958 prices remained stable at about $3 per barrel. In March 1971 the balance of power shifted – the month that the Texas Railroad commission set proporation (a formula to distribute quotas of oil production per operator thereby artificially maintaining price levels) at 100 per cent for the first time there was no limit on oil production. They were pioneers of the technique to keep the price of oil artificially high by restricting production of oil producers in America. The Arabs were then to deploy the same technique.

In March 1971 the price of oil was $3, by 1974 oil had quadrupled. The Yom Kippur War of Syria and Egypt against Israel started on October 5, 1973. The USA and Western countries supported Israel and the Arab nations supported Egypt and Syria. OPEC, which had been formed in 1960, imposed an oil embargo whereby the Arab nations curtailed the production of crude oil by five million barrels a day. The ability to control the world price of crude oil had shifted from the USA to OPEC.[3]

The Arab sheiks (rulers) who had formed OPEC soon discovered that oil was more valuable left underground, and limited its supply until its price was hiked.

Towards a national miners' union

Prior to the great Miners Federation leaders, there were religious non-conformist leaders, such as William Abrahams 'Mabon' ('The Bard' known for his marvellous public speaking skills) – Mabon became the first president of the South Wales Miners' Federation in 1907, and professed a more liberal approach - he eventually became a Liberal MP. It was a period of an alliance with Labour called Lib-Lab that saw Abrahams win seven successive elections as Liberal MP before retiring in 1920. He urged a more accommodating approach towards the coal owners' quest for profits, preaching weekly from the pulpits for restraint and peaceful protest and negotiation.

These men of Liberal politics and religious zeal didn't leave the stage of trade union and Labour history lightly.

It took a more radical movement of men, meeting in inconspicuous circum-stances in the nooks and crannies of the mine, the local pubs, the mountainside or even in one another's parlours (as small as they were) to organise and to establish a new kind of radical leadership among the miners.

These men were accused of interfering in matters they knew little about. To go to another colliery to canvass opinion was a crime in the eyes of the then established lodge leaderships. Little had changed in parts of the South Wales Coalfield by the time of the momentous strike of 1984-85.

As a result of these struggles towards the end of the 19th Century, the Labour Party was born in 1906, preceded by the Labour Representation Committee formed in 1900 - a body which succeeded in getting the Scottish miners' leader Keir Hardie elected as the first recognisable Labour MP in Merthyr in 1900. He had previously been elected as Independent Labour Party MP for West Ham in 1892 but lost his seat in 1895.

The Miners Federation in the Maesteg District

In the Llynfi Valley area, Vernon Hartshorne established himself as a famous local and South Wales Miners leader between 1900 and his death in 1931. He rose to become Postmaster General in the MacDonald minority Labour Government of 1929-31.

Peter Stead (Glamorgan Historian 1969, reproduced in the Maesteg Town Hall Centenary Pamphlet 1981) wrote of Hartshorne: *"In the field of industrial relations, Mr Hartshorne's fame came mainly through his work on the SWMF Executive. His early days on the body were full of the verbal battles which dominated most meetings; but eventually ousting his rivals to emerge in the years before 1905 as one of the key men on the executive. As well as wages and conditions, which he was mainly interested in, it was the fact that he took the lead in negotiations... Mr Hartshorne was quite militant but never extreme. Journalists who met him were always apparently quite surprised to find he was not the wild talking firebrand they had been led to expect."*

There is a further analysis on Vernon Hartshorne's life in my Ruskin College thesis (1978): History of Mining in Llynfi and Afan Valleys. (Available from the Afan Argoed, Afan Valley, museum website).

An obituary for Hartshorne was written in the Times on Wednesday, March 18, 1931. Thousands attended his funeral to his place of burial in Llangynwyd Church, Maesteg. His local reputation had obviously remained strong throughout the years of the depression in Wales.

Union organising in the 1970s and 1980s

This account will explain how, in not too dissimilar circumstances, I participated in a struggle in the NUM both in the UK and Wales This was a struggle for the hearts and minds of miners - entreating them to participate in intelligent methods of organising to achieve a more socialist and militant leadership among the rank and file and within the structures of the NUM to defend miners' jobs and standards of living.

It saw young miners challenging the old ways of doing things; challenging the way that the lodge, area and national leaders had opted for lifetime appointments as union officials and rewrote the rule books and determined the pay and conditions via the executive councils that they ran to legitimise the practice.

Young miners, instead, called for the implementation of the principles of trade union representative democracy, which has its constraints as well as its virtues and privileges and honour in representing working people.

The Thatcher government imposed regular election of full-time officials as a means to try to keep the officials and trade unions in check. This was one of their quirky bits of legislation not necessarily consistent with their Conservative philosophy.

Behind it, also, was the fact that they were nervous about left-wing candidates winning elections in trade unions as lifetime appointments - as happened in the TGWU with Jack Jones, and Hugh Scanlon's election as president of the AUEW. These men were to become influential trade union leaders particularly in shaping government incomes policies as was the case with the Social Contract under the Harold Wilson government 1963 to 1970.

Later, leaders such as Joe Marino of the Bakers Union and left-wing candidates in the teachers unions and civil service unions were emerging as intelligent champions of the workers' position. The rank and file wanted regular elections for the same reasons to make their full-time officials accountable to them.

Many NUM officials, elected or appointed before the 1970s, or in the wake of the two national miners' strikes in 1972 and 1974, had established left-wing credentials.[4]

But many when in office opted mainly for the status quo or went along with the upsurge in direct action and calls for equipping the men to take on the challenges of the National Coal Board in terms of knowledge and research.

However, there began to emerge policies of resistance to colliery closures: demands for regular elections of full-time officials, as well as the traditional demands for miners to retire at 55 after a lifetime in mining and to have a decent wage in terms of parity with the highest-paid industrial workers.

A new Miners' Broad Left

Many young miners began to join a forum called the Miners' Broad Left formed by Militant supporters and other left-wing groups and non-affiliated militant miners in 1979 by rank-and-file miners from South Wales, Scotland, Northumberland, Durham and Yorkshire. While publishing a widely circulated programme for defending the mining industry, they also opposed the "parity" policy of the TUC, which provided for full-time union officers having the same salaries as their counterparts in management, who they negotiated with on a national or area basis.

In the 1980s, the pay of full-time officials in the South Wales area was twice that of a face worker on full underground rate.

So, how could they in all consciousness fight hard for the ordinary miner when their personal demands as leaders had already been met and more after the NUM introduced company cars and other allowances?[5]

1 Source Opencast Coalmining Statistics 2008 – 'Minerals UK' website.
2 A J Cook, 1883 -1931, a pamphlet by Paul Davies, A J Cook Memorial Committee Bristol. Head of History, Mortimer Comprehensive School, Alfreton, Derbyshire.
3 History and Analysis – Crude Oil prices, James L Williams, WTRG Economics. Arkansas. © 1996-2007
4 For a more in-depth analysis of the role of the trade union leaders in the 1970 and 1980s, I would refer the reader to Ken Smith's Book, A Civil War without Guns – Socialist Publications, 2004.
5 There also existed at this time "The Left" as it was called, which was in reality a small group of full-time officials around the Communist Party of Great Britain, facilitated by Professor Vic Allen of Sheffield University. This will be referred to later.

St John's Colliery from the North

2 Countdown to the 1984-85 strike

What things looked like as the strike loomed.

I N 1984 St John's Colliery nestled in the slopes of Cwmdu, below a grassed over slagheap above the town of Maesteg. There had been two tips shaped like black pyramids. They were levelled off into one tip for safety reasons in the late 1970s. It was the last remaining colliery in the Llynfi Valley. St John's Colliery was known to miners and their families as Cwmdu.

In 1979, Caerau Colliery had closed with men transferred to Coegnant Colliery and St John's, with some going to pits as far away as Wyndham Western in the Ogmore Valley. In 1982 Coegnant Colliery then closed with men transferring to St John's and men transferring to pits as far away as Cwm and Coedely in the Llantrisant area.

St John's colliery found itself with 960 men on its books in 1983, and by the time of the start of the miners' strike in March 1984 there were still over 900 men on books.

This number of men was more than the pit's operations could reasonably sustain. Men were led to believe that they were being kept together in these numbers in order to meet the manning requirements of the new mine that the NCB was rumoured to be planning to open in Margam near the former Aberbaiden Colliery. This "planned" Margam New mine had been on and off the starter's blocks since 1973.

To this day (2009), it has a power supply and the beginnings of a slant to open as a horizon mining colliery – cutting deep across the seams and working from the top down under the Margam Mountain near Pyle and Port Talbot.

Speculation persisted during 2009 that Tata, the Indian conglomerate which had bought out Corus the Dutch Steel Makers, was going to open the Margam Coal reserves.

Margam – A new mine?

S t John's NUM had a long association with the prospect of a Margam new mine. During the 1983 strike, which started when Lewis Merthyr was earmarked for closure on March 1 that year, some miners from St John's broke into the local NCB Miners Agent's office in Tondu and retrieved the NCB plans for opening the Margam new mine.

These plans had been in place since 1973. The material was photocopied and placed back in the NCB Agent's Office. We conducted a media campaign urging the NCB to begin opening the Margam mine to enable St John's men to transfer in the event that the pit might be exhausted in 10 years' time.

Who said miners weren't forward looking in their vision for the future of their jobs and families?

Paul Starling was an enlightened journalist working for HTV Wales News - the local ITV region serving Wales in the 1980s - who went beyond his normal brief in putting himself out to help St John's NUM in trying to establish the truth about the Margam new mine. Paul, a former journalist on the Oxford Mail who became a presenter with HTV conducted a number of in-depth interviews with Maesteg miners and produced investigative journalist type presentations of the miners' issues on HTV news and other programmes before and during the miners' strike. I shall always be appreciative of his candour and approach to these issues, and indeed it must have taken a personal toll in terms of his own commitment to the truth of what was happening at the time. Paul went on later to be a founder member of the Bevan Society in Wales, with Aberavon MP Hywel Francis. The struggle for justice sometimes consumes every fibre of an individual's principles and commitment. Paul did that.

Mining: A way of life

I was born in Neath General Hospital. My parents lived in Duffryn Rhondda. My father worked as an underground haulage driver in Duffryn Colliery.

My parents had taken myself, my brother and sister as young children from Croeserw in the Afan Valley to Oxford in the summer of 1960. My father had studied at Ruskin College from 1958 and then chose to find work in the Cowley car works in preference to returning to the coal mine at Duffryn Rhondda.

In April 1974, I returned home to Wales after having taken part in the "mutuality" strike at Cowley for ten weeks. I had no money for rent, or enough to send home to my parents, who were looking after my son, Owain, who was then aged three.

I resigned my position as a shop steward and handed in my notice at Cowley. After a short time working at Borg Warner and Silent Channel, I started work in St John's at the end of the miners' holiday in August 1974. My return to Maesteg, after my father was made redundant from the Cowley car works in Oxford, was full of memories of my great grandfather, Maurice (known as Morris), and grandfather, Emlyn, who had been overmen and deputies in the local mines of Caerau, Duffryn Rhondda and St John's.

These men had been in charge of safety and production in the various districts of the mines. I recently found out that my great grandfather on my mother's side, John

Ambrose, had also worked in the collieries around Blaengarw and Llangeinor in 1900 to 1910. This is just five miles east of Maesteg where the Garw valley joins the Llynfi Valley itself. In fact, my Grandfather William John Ambrose was born in Llangeinor at the foot of the Garw valley.

Following a month in a surface training workshop, which simulated underground conditions called the galleries at Tondu, I then trained underground in St John's Colliery with Mel Wills and Danny (Bibles) Evans. Mel has been a friend of mine for many years swapping stories of our times together years ago as we enjoy a pint in our local Maesteg Workingmen's Club. I became friends with Ivor Collier, fire officer at St John's, and his friend 'Long' John Jones who was a dust suppression officer at the pit. Both have been chairmen of the local Workingman's club of which I am a member of to this day. I joined in 1977. My uncle John Isaac and 'Long' John signed my application forms for membership. Ivor Collier would see me at the pit or in club on Saturday afternoon and tell me stories of how he was a card carrying member of the Communist Party and had participated in the 'Boys Strike' in St John's Colliery during the war. It was a dispute over the payment of 'trumps' whereby the collier would pay his assistant and teenage collier boy out of his own pay packet which included bonus earned as a result of the boy's efforts. Many boys would find themselves searching the pubs and clubs in the valley for their collier to ask for their 'trumps', a demeaning practice, that many boys resented but had to put up with. The strike helped to put paid to such a practice even though Ivor and his friends were fined by local magistrates for unlawful strike action at a time of war.

I also trained with Ron (Spanner) Thomas in the G36 and G38 coal faces. After obtaining my underground certificates to work on the coalface, successfully completing my "improvership" with Nigel Taylor from Glyncorrwg, I worked on the M11, G40, G41, G42 coal faces. To train as a miner you had to work 40 days in a surface training complex. There was one nearby in Tondu in the Galleries, as they were described, where there was a simulated mining environment with classrooms and a canteen.

After 100 days as a trainee with a fully qualified miner in a coalface designated as a training face, which also produced coal in the normal way except that a number of trainees would be in the face working alongside the colliers, there was then a 40-day improvership where you could work on your own but supervised by the district deputy or underground official.

A chance for a mature student period of study

A few years after starting at St John's, I applied to Ruskin College in Oxford, which was a trade union college for mature students.

To gain entry, I wrote an essay on the need for co-operation among the international trade union movement in the face of the growth of multinational conglomerates, which were increasingly dominating world trade and commodity prices. I was then offered a place in Ruskin on a TUC bursary. This had been my second attempt to gain a place at the college. On my first attempt, I wrote an essay on workers' control and management of the mining industry.

I have often wondered why this wasn't acceptable to the Ruskin College selection panel at the time. I was fascinated why the coal mines - a nationalised industry - still wasn't fulfilling its potential to be a model of workers' participation under modern conditions of production.

While the industry had suffered under private ownership, it had been the subject of a government inquiry. The Sankey Commission in 1921 recommended a seven-hour day and an increase in wages. It also recommended immediate implementation of its interim recommendations in July 1921 - initially to avert a national strike over hours and pay.

It also recommended the nationalisation of an industry that was suffering from a terrible safety record, horrendous working conditions and lack of technology in its operations compared to other mining industries abroad and in the Soviet Union.

These recommendations were undone in 1926 by the Samuel Commission under the Tory Government. It took until 1947 for the nationalisation of the mines to be carried through - a demand that had been campaigned for by A J Cook and others throughout the 1920s and 1930s.

So how then did this industry finally become nationalised in 1947, when there were flags hoisted in the pits declaring: "This pit is run by the NCB on behalf of the nation".

After a few short years, those flags were allowed to be shred by the winds until the wooden flagpoles were recycled into stick for the fire.

This was more than a physical phenomena, it represented the deteriorating state of the industry. Why was this happening? This was one of the reasons I went to Ruskin College, to find out!

I had read Page Arnott's histories of the miners. He was an exceptionally diligent historian and scholar of the miners' union. If such an eye for detail was used, by those now claiming to be historians, to describe the history of mining following nationalisation in 1947, we would all be the better off for understanding why the industry was allowed to be sacrificed at the political altar of successive governments' lack of an energy policy'.

In the case of the Tories this was also bound up with an additional, more class-conscious aim, to emasculate and destroy the miners' unions as a first step towards emasculating the rest of the British trade union movement.

More than £9 billion was spent by various wings of government and the state during the 1984-85 miners' strike to defeat the miners. It was the largest operation of "quantitative easing", or perhaps we should call it "counterfeiting" that was to be carried out by any government until the "credit crunch" and "banking crisis" of 2008/09. Andrew Glyn estimated that total cost of the miners' strike was £5 billion by Christmas of 1984, "when all hidden costs, including loss of output, taxation, increased social security payments are taken into account". Those events were a long way off as I recall picking up my Ruskin Diploma in Social Studies having read industrial sociology, politics and economics after two years as a full-time student.

Another election

In 1977, I stood for president of the Mature Students Union (MSU) which was a student's association affiliated to the National Students Union (NUS) that represented the six adult residential colleges: Ruskin, Fircroft, Surbiton, Coleg Harlech, Northern College, Barnsley and Bourneville College, Birmingham. For me, it was a means to sharpen the tools of organising, agitating and educating students about their rights.

It was a one-year appointment that I took seriously enough - reading its history and chairing its meetings in various parts of the country.

I can honestly say that this bit of "virtual" trade unionism" resulted in the abolition of the age limit on students' railcards.

Mature students had been denied the right to subsidised rail travel unless under the age of 25. By abolishing the age limit all students of all ages could enjoy the same rights.

We also retained the privileges at that time of two free travel warrants home as part of our mature students grant from the Department for Education. We also campaigned for a full time sabbatical officer for the MSU which I'm told was granted three years later.

As president, one of my first duties was to meet Prime Minister James Callaghan MP (1976-1979). `

Callaghan started what was to become known in education circles as the great debate when he spoke at Ruskin College about the legitimate concerns of the public about education in maintained schools which led 10 years later to the establishment of the National Curriculum under the Conservative Government of Margaret Thatcher.

On behalf of the Ruskin Students Union, myself and National Secretary Marie Van Helmond representing the National Mature Students Union, met James Callaghan and his retinue of Special Branch officers in the students' quarter at The Rookery, Headington, and Oxford. He was due to lay the foundation stone on a new student accommodation block. We had a chat, and a cup of tea, and an exchange of views about the needs of mature students.

On taking him to the foundation stone - that had a kind of scaffold holding it over a hole dug for the purpose - I could see out of the corner of my eye that one of the students had pinned a large placard to the scaffold which read: "Jim loves Julian more than he loves Splott."

This was a reference to Callaghan's close "friendship" with Julian Hodge the managing director of the Bank of Wales. The protest headlined in the Daily Telegraph with the photo of the placard the following day!

During my time at college, I was allowed to work in St John's Colliery during the summer and Easter holidays. With a family to look after I needed the extra money to top-up the mature student grant. My son, Owain, was just two years old when I first worked underground. He was by now five years old.

At Easter 1978, Phil Stafford who had held the post as St John's NUM Lodge Secretary from 1954 decided he would retire. He was 66 years of age by that time.

I had quite a lot of support among the men in the colliery at the time for my views and opinions, and many a time a miner would encourage me to sit down over a pinch of snuff and engage in discussions about the union or the political and current affairs of the time.

Standing for office

I was proposed and seconded for the position of lodge secretary with three other candidates. With four candidates standing, I received 56 per cent of the total vote - this was enough to win the ballot outright. The vote being 365 for myself and with 190, 80 and eight for the other candidates.

One of the candidates later became one of my best friends, a man who embraced rather than resented my success in becoming lodge secretary – the most prized position in the Lodge. Ron Roberts who later became vice-chairman of St John's and the ablest treasurer during the 1984-85 strike has always proved himself a man of great trustworthiness, honesty and tact.

For me, the election as lodge secretary was the beginning of a baptism of fire, a blaze that would burn and not go out for 10 years of struggle to advance the cause of the NUM and Keep Mining in Maesteg. It was the start of my 'ten-year stint', a lot different to the one

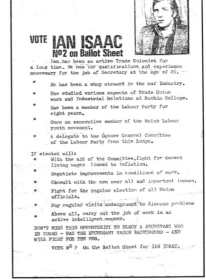

VOTE **IAN ISAAC**
Nº2 on Ballot Sheet

Ian has been an active Trade Unionist for a long time. He has the qualifications and experience necessary for the job of Secretary at the age of 26.

* He has been a shop steward in the car Industry.
* Has studied various aspects of Trade Union work and Industrial Relations at Ruskin College.
* Has been a member of the Labour Party for eight years.
* Once an executive member of the Welsh Labour youth movement.
* A delegate to the Ogmore General Committee of the Labour Party from this Lodge.

If elected will:
* With the aid of the Committee, fight for decent living wages linked to inflation.
* Negotiate improvements in conditions of work.
* Consult with the men over all and important issues.
* Fight for the regular election of all Union officials.
* Pay regular visits underground to discuss problems
* Above all, carry out the job of work in an active intelligent manner.

DON'T MISS THIS OPPORTUNITY TO ELECT A SECRETARY WHO IS YOUNG - HAS THE NECESSARY UNION BACKGROUND - AND WILL FIGHT FOR THE MEN.

VOTE Nº 2 On the Ballot Sheet for IAN ISAAC.

that Alf Robens went through. From 1978 to 1988 I was to serve as an official both locally and on the South Wales Area Executive Council of the NUM.

After the pithead ballot

I had been elected at the age of 26 as full-time lodge secretary for life in a ballot held at the colliery in April 1978. I took up my position on July 3, 1978, after collecting my Ruskin College Oxford, Social Studies Diploma.

I had been offered a place to study law in Aberystwyth. After attending the university to meet the head of the law faculty, I was invited to matriculate in October 1978.

After much family debate, I decided that I had already been away from home enough and I would opt to work as a trade union organiser, putting into practice some of the lessons I had learnt in college. I recalled what Karl Marx had said "conditions determine consciousness".

Mining was, after all, in my blood and a big part of my consciousness. In many respects, the men expected me to have a go – it was why I went to college - they thought. The fact that the NCB local management and industrial relations department thought I would pursue a career in industrial relations for the Coal Board was another matter.

I didn't flinch at opting for the NUM rather than the NCB.

I was young; miners didn't normally become NUM officials until they were in their 40s (you were classed as a boy until then). And apart from union experience with three years as a shop steward in British Leyland Cowley, Oxford, between 1971 and 1973, I still had a lot to learn about the mining industry itself.

Within a matter of months I had to learn the techniques of representing the interests of the men while being confronted with a difficult, and at times impossible, industrial relations climate created by the policies of the Coal Board. These became even more acute with the insidious stranglehold on the industry created by the newly elected Tory Government in May 1979 - reflected in lack of support, lower investment and rundown of the industry with a growing number of pit closures.

Peter Walker, the Tory Energy Minister (1983-1987), was to be the one responsible for the policies of the Tory Cabinet of Margaret Thatcher in respect of energy and the mining industry in the 1980s. He had been dismissed by Thatcher when she took over as Tory leader in 1975 because he disagreed publicly with her social and economic policies.

Although classed as a Tory "Wet" he was to be readmitted into Thatcher's cabinet. This former president of the Young Conservatives caused Margaret Thatcher much frustration through his lack of zeal in pursuing the inner cabinet policy of reducing the mining industry and the destruction of the NUM. For all that, Peter Walker would become Welsh Secretary from 1987 to 1990 and was given his reward in 1992, being elevated to the House of Lords as Baron Walker of Worcester, a constituency he had been MP for from 1961 to 1992.

Peter Walker's role as Secretary of State for Energy was to amount to no more than presiding over the buffet at the funeral. Miners would be offered no compulsory redundancy provided they transfer to other mines and men aged 50 and over could retire on pension of £35 a week which was the equivalent of a shifts pay per week in 1981/82. To participate in the funeral of your pit for a shift a week for the rest of your life - what a choice!

In stark contrast politically to Peter Walker, Nicholas Ridley was a Thatcherite ("one of us" said Margaret Thatcher), a member of the Selsdon Group. He had published a strategy paper in 1978, before the Tories came to power, that to all intents and purposes proposed a long funeral for the mining industry as a means of destroying the foundations of trade unionism in the UK. His recommendations were leaked to The Economist on May 27, 1978, nearly five years before the miners' strike. Ridley suggested contingency planning in order to defeat any challenge from the unions. He outlined how the next Conservative Government (Thatcher was elected in May 1979) could fight, and defeat, a major strike in a nationalised industry.

The plan included:

- The Government should if possible choose the field of battle
- Industries were grouped together by the likelihood of winning a strike; the coal industry was in the 'middle of the three groups of industries mentioned.
- Coal stocks to be built up at power stations
- Plans should be made to import coal from non-union foreign ports
- Non-union lorry drivers to be recruited by haulage companies
- Dual coal-oil firing generators to be installed, at great extra cost
- Cut off the money supply to the strikers and make the union finance them
- Train and equip a large, mobile squad of police, ready to employ riot tactics in order to uphold the law against violent picketing.

The interests of capital and the state combine

Referring to the 1980s without even a mention of the miners' strikes, Margaret Thatcher in a memorial lecture commemorating "Nick", offered her assessment of the success of her strategy as she saw it: *The important point is that the 'overall strategy' we* [the Conservative Government or 'we' meaning herself and Ridley, my emphasis] *pursued in the 1980s worked precisely as it was meant to. And it transformed the reality and the reputation of Britain. Moreover, it was a strategy. It was not a set of policies cobbled together from minute to minute, begged, borrowed or stolen from other people. It was successful because it was based on clear, firmly held*

principles which were themselves based on a right understanding of politics, econom-
ics and above all human nature.

"Nick enjoyed high office, but he was usually surprised to be offered it. I think he
had rather given up on entering the Cabinet when I appointed him to transport in
1984. I wish I had brought him in earlier. He would have been a superb Chancellor.

"For there was a strong paternalistic streak in the Conservative Party when Nick
and I entered politics; and it was something both of us disliked. The Tory paternalists
were well-intentioned, of course, but because economics was below them – and
philosophy beyond them – the main impact of Tory Governments was to legitimise
and consolidate socialism.

"Nick never hesitated to oppose the statism of post-war Conservatives as consis-
tently as that of the Labour Party. From the backbenches after 1972 he aimed his
barbs of unwelcome – because unanswerable – criticism at those who had fallen away
from the verities of Selsdon Man (and woman). For Nick it must have seemed a
thankless, hopeless, sojourn in a wilderness populated by prowling whips and sharp-
toothed party managers. But had he and others not then stayed true to their beliefs, I
am not sure that we could have later turned the party round."[1]

Life at the pit

Colliery managers come and go, but the body politic of the miners and their unions lived on in the mores, cultures, customs and practices of different collieries. St John's was no different to many of the other 34 collieries in South Wales that were open at the time in 1978. Yet, St John's Lodge NUM was as different as other collieries and their union leaderships were different. Personalities were involved, interpretations of the definitions of power, democracy, the right to represent people: the philosophy of socialism and how to affect change towards a goal of a fairer society. This was the bread and butter of day to day mining and trade union existence. It was a play enacted in real time for the heart and soul of the mining communities.

These differences in the relative balance of power between union lodge and Coal Board management, on a day-to-day basis, were sometimes mercilessly exploited at times of crisis.

The penny began to drop as it had never dropped before: the trick or technique of the NCB for closing collieries was to manipulate colliery outputs, give them second-hand machinery, or give them new machinery for a short period and replace it with old stock, and then charge the total cost of the new machinery on the previous colliery accounts. The new machinery would then be transferred to another colliery as depreciated stock. A combination of manipulations by NCB accountants and mining engineers, consciously, by inclination or otherwise, was to run a pit down, blame the men for lack of performance, create industrial relations problems in a pit and blame absenteeism (which in some pits reached 20 per cent of the workforce).

When older miners transferred from pit to pit, the knock-on effect was for the average age to increase, the number of lung-diseased, disabled and ill miners increased, and this in turn affected absenteeism. All these insidious propaganda methods were aimed at wearing down the resistance of miners, resulting in them voting for the closure of their own colliery.

These methods were aimed at wearing the men down so that they became what Welsh miners refer to as "danted". This pitched miner against miner and undermined solidarity.

When it came to the judgement day, the NCB would call the colliery in for review to the NCB HQ in Llanishen, Cardiff. Llanishen was known as the biggest pit in Wales, because of the number of white-collar staff working there. The cost of running this uneconomic administrative centre was divided equally between each colliery unit. As collieries closed, the fewer collieries the more overheads dumped on to the costs of the remaining pits. Today it is a leisure centre.

St John's Lodge Committee - 1978-79

Standing—W. Lloyd, Paul Davies, Roy Davies, Wayne Morgan, Ivor Collier, Tudor Hembrow, J. Jones
Seated—Ray Barnard, Thos. Bumford, Ron Roberts (*Vice-Chairman*), Thos. Kearle (*Chairman*), Ian Isaac (*Secretary*), Harold Phillips, Norman Dawkins

The accounting knock-on effects managed to distribute the area costs to remaining pits, thereby dumping disproportionate costs on to the remaining pits.[2]

They then stated that the colliery would have to close because of bad geology, unworkable coal seams and end of year losses amounting to several millions of pounds (most of it dumped onto a colliery's accounts by an accountant's pen).

The NUM lodge officers and a lodge committee of about 12 men of affected pits were given their fate in a mahogany-clad board room in Llanishen, Cardiff. This happened to St John's Lodge NUM in March 1982 and again in June 1985.

The lodge immediately registered an appeal to the next stage to the new colliery review procedure, which took place in Hobart House, the Coal Board HQ in London.

A modified version of this colliery review procedure was to become the basis of an "agreement" between Nacods (Deputies Union) and the NCB to end the 1984 miners' strike. The NUM went back to work without an agreement and this was to become an ironic factor on our ability to proceed to a judge in chambers at the end of the fight to keep St John's open.

How they closed pits

When a pit was being reviewed by the area board, because its production was not covering the cost of overheads as determined by the NCB accountants, the NUM lodge committee would then have to call a general meeting to inform the men of the terms offered by the coal board, redundancy or transfer or vote to fight the closure. Nine times out of 10 the deed was done.

The men by then were either advised by the lodge committee to fight on or had become "danted" and voted to accept the NCB terms thereby agreeing to close the mine. You can imagine the expletives of angry frustrated men as they walked away from the final meeting that meant the closure of their pit, a workplace that for many had spanned decades.

This kind of scene had been repeated in most mining communities, with few exceptions, since the 1950s. During the 1950s, 60s and 70s it could always be argued that there was always another pit to transfer to or other work available in the economy.

Those on the right wing of the Labour and trade union movement could always have the luxury of burying their head in the sand. Union leaders, such as NUM president Joe Gormley, would preside over pits closing in the same way that a Bishop would preside over his local clergy conducting funerals in the communities.

From afar at the NUM's Euston Road HQ, *"all they were concerned with was to give the pit a decent burial"* was the way Terry Thomas, NUM Miners Agent for the Maesteg and Swansea District, once described the process with some irony.

Local government councillors and MPs became accustomed to the force of argument by the NUM in favour of fighting to retain jobs and communities put forward by left wingers in the mines and elsewhere. But they could always then breathe a sigh of relief when a pit shut, leaving them to proceed unhindered with their careers in local government and the Labour Party.

They would even utter outrageous statements seeking cheap personal publicity. One infamous phrase was that uttered by electricians' union leader Eric Hammond at the height of the 1984-85 miners' strike at the 1984 TUC, where he said that the miners were "lions led by donkeys". This phrase originates from the First World War to describe the thousands of troops led to premature deaths in the French and Belgian trenches.

This phrase was to be brought out as a retread by Jeff Jones, a former council leader, in a 20th anniversary article about the strike in the Glamorgan Gazette covering Bridgend and Maesteg.

This refrain was always attempting to put across that the coal mines closed because of the tactics adopted by the NUM and its leaders! This couldn't be further from the truth as will be explained more fully during the course of this account.

Yet, these were the very people who had turned their backs on the problems faced by mining communities during the 1960s and 70s, a bad habit they were to persist with during and after the strike of 1984-85.

Jeff Jones was never seen on a picket line or at any event that supported miners during the strike. If he did anything it was for 'show' only.

Every pit community had a Jeff Jones, someone who had had a little mature student education and went on to become right-wing opponents of the miners' lodges. It was their dress rehearsal for their support for the 'New Labour' project of Neil Kinnock, Tony Blair and Peter Mandelson in the 1990s

I witnessed this up and down the British coalfield before and during the strike of 1984. These individuals were smug and above the struggle of ordinary workers when they became appointed full-time council leaders.

Later in the 1990s, when council leaders were paid through the local authority cabinet structures they were to become even more remote from the realities of community life despite the fact they were elected to represent residents' interests on the council.

Pit closures a constant statistic

A very important fact bears out the political nature of the rundown of the mining industry following nationalisation in 1947. In every year from 1947, an average of six collieries were closed in Britain's coalfield according to the NCB's Year Book from 1948 to 1994 [the year of privatisation of the coal industry] - the exceptions were the years that miners had gone on strike or had overtime bans or industrial action against pit closures.

The years when more than nine were closed came after the 1984-85 miners' strike. The pit closure programme accelerated further when Government policies gave preference in market terms to other kinds of fuels used in the economy or when manufacturing industry contracted due to high inflation, recession or a high value to the pound. With less manufacturing there was less demand for coal.

Britain's share of world manufacturing trade had been slashed from 25 per cent after the Second World War to less than seven per cent. by 1984. Starting a year later, 92 collieries were to close between April 1985 and December 1989 (Source Alphabetical List of NCB/British Coal collieries 1947-1995 – list originally issued in April 1992 by HQ finance dept, Eastwood Hall Nottingham)

When I started work in the mining industry in1974, there were 33 collieries in the South Wales Coalfield. Twelve collieries in the South Wales coalfield were to be closed from 1978 to the start of the miners' strike on March 12, 1984, when only 21 pits remained in the South Wales Area.

Mining is an extractive industry. In other words, you extract the mineral from the available seams and then you exhaust the mine of winnable coal.

Miners have always understood this. When a pit was exhausted, it would be acceptable to organise its closure. But if it was closed leaving millions of tonnes of winnable coal then this was hard to swallow, especially when jobs were becoming scarce in the British economy in the 1980s.

The NCB were closing pits for uneconomic reasons (so they argued) rather than proven exhaustion of reserves of coal. In some cases pits were closed after millions of pounds of investment had been put in, as was the case with Duffryn Rhondda. The pit had sunk one of its shafts deeper in order to access fresh coal reserves in 1963 and then closed in 1965.

Learning the lessons and preparing for the struggles ahead

St John's NUM Lodge had begun to learn the lessons of other colliery closures. In the past it had been sufficient for the lodge leaders and the committee to be concerned with not much more than little local difficulties from time to time on an industrial relations level, mainly sorting out discrepancies over pay and dealing with compensation, house coal and other local matters.

If a colliery in the next valley closed, then that was seen as the next valley's problem. People would empathise and commiserate and that would suffice. Miners would, at that time, have had the option of transferring to another pit up the road. If an NUM lodge from another valley appealed for a vote for strike action throughout the coalfield against closure of their colliery, (as was the case at Afan Ocean Colliery, Abergwynfi, in 1968), ways and means and arguments were found in conferences and in prominent opinion amongst lodge officials to decline support and vote against.

St John's Lodge had done this in 1968, with its lodge leaders voting against supporting Afan Ocean Colliery in the next valley over, the Afan Valley. Verbatim accounts are contained in the South Wales NUM section of Swansea University's Archive of the South Wales Coalfield. Also the 'Fed' written by Hywel Francis and Dai Smith covers the closure of Afan Ocean. The new St John's leadership in 1978 was determined that such a situation like that would never happen again.

Lodge leaderships in St John's pre-1978 had represented the men well enough given the circumstances of the time. Will Thomas had been secretary during the war and Ernie Watkins, a local Communist Party member, was de facto secretary well into the 1950s when Phil Stafford, a local Labour councillor and member of the local water board, took over in 1954. As well as support from mainstream Labour members, he also had the support of the local Roman Catholic priest who it is said publicly canvassed for him at the time from the pulpit. Such outside influence from other sections of society was commonplace in the mining industry.

The mines and their miners were, after all, part of the communities they were in. The activities and operations of the mine was the core of conversation when miners, their families and friends met for a drink or met one and other in the town, in church or chapel or in the street. Yet, none of these past NUM lodge committees, secretaries, or their chairmen had looked very far beyond their own patch for answers to the pit's problems.

Of course, the folklore of individual disgruntlement with the quality of representation came up among the miners from time to time, but no one had lost their job except for reasons of gross misconduct and these were few and far between.

Men would say it was a waste of time calling in the lodge office, "they do nothing for you anyway". I committed myself to turn around this sense of alienation from the lodge leadership among its rank and file.

The NUM nationally had negotiated a national conciliation agreement, where consultation committees met to discuss operational, production and health and safety matters, allowing the union to achieve a reputation for resolving conflict through the industrial relations channels via this conciliation agreement.

Will Paynter, a Welshman from the Rhondda, had negotiated the power loading agreement in 1966 as president of the national union.

The 1966 power loading agreement tended to resolve the conflicts between job descriptions and rates of pay and coal production was based on co-operation and not payment by results, which had been the case in the past.

Will Paynter, before becoming president of the NUM had been a member of the Communist Party and who had participated in the hunger marches of the 1930s. In the 1960s he had been responsible for establishing the power loading agreement and worked tirelessly for better pay and conditions for mineworkers within the industry.

I saw Will Paynter speak at a South Wales Miners Library weekend school in the late 1970s. He conveyed powerful images of the conditions of the miners and working people during the 1920s and 30s. His voice resonated with the grit of all those years of struggle. I had also spoken to Idris Cox a former Maesteg/Garth/Merthyr Colliery Miner who had been blacklisted in the mines in the 1930s, who was to become the editor of The Daily Worker, the forerunner of The Morning Star, the daily newspaper of the Communist Party. Idris, retired and living in Porthcawl, was by then in his 80s – a polite, quietly spoken man whose interests were rekindled by the public meetings organised in the Maesteg Town Hall to raise awareness about job losses in industry.

By 1971, a uniform national shift rate had been agreed for men working underground. The number of job descriptions had been reduced drastically from 150 down to 30. The industry had established a quaint way of running itself for generations in terms of job descriptions.

For a while, men worked on a level playing field irrespective of the conditions for winning coal easily or not. They were on the same rate of pay. This had been hard won by the NUM during the 1960s and 70s.

The President becomes a Lord

By 1978 circumstances had changed. With Joe Gormley as president of the NUM, the NCB introduced an incentive agreement based on bonus payments for increased coal production. This put area against area and men against men.

There had been a national ballot on the incentive scheme which resulted in a No vote. However, the then national president convinced the union's right-wing national executive committee to vote in favour of area ballots. The introduction of the incentive scheme was bitterly resisted by St John's Lodge, as it was by the South Wales miners as a whole.

By 1978 the die was cast, and we had no option but to attempt to live with it and negotiate incentive agreements continually every time a coalface opened or a drive way to develop roadways and coal faces was undertaken.

Colliery managers wanted more yardage (distance travelled in excavating roadways or coal seams), and the men with the support of the NUM Lodge wanted less yardage, indeed they wanted better rates of bonus for the distances travelled. This was a bitter source of conflict that constantly took up lodge officials and committeemens' time. Joe Gormley, national president until 1982, eventually became a Lord under the Thatcher Government, He also became chairman of the Tote, a Government on-course betting syndicate, one can only guess why!

It was common knowledge that different pits in the South Wales area had different incentive agreements. Some agreements (based on a predetermined template introduced by the Coal Board in the last days of the Joe Gormley presidency in 1981). Were easy to achieve - resulting in more bonuses in the pay packet. Some were less achievable, resulting in fewer bonuses paid out if any.

This became a root cause of much discontent in the coalfield and had the propensity to put miner against miner, with stories abounding of good bonuses in some pits and men in the poorest-paid pits blaming their own leaders for unachievable targets. Managers could of course exploit this situation and placed much added pressure on lodge committees and NUM lodge officers. It was no accident that the pits with the poorest incentive agreements appeared to be the ones earmarked for closure. By 1982, St John's had soaked up all the available manpower in the area that it could cope with, and was in constant conflict with the St John's Colliery Manager over the poor incentive agreements on offer.

The following extract from Wikipedia illustrates the opinions felt about Joe Gormley's term of office as president of the NUM (1971-1982). It followed a BBC programme in 2002.

"One of Gormley's long-term impacts that affected the 1984-85 strike was his role in the wage reforms of 1977. The reforms paid miners a wage proportionate to the output of their region. This gave the Nottinghamshire miners the highest wages of all and they were very reluctant to go on strike in 1984, when none of their pits were under threat and they had high wages to lose.

Another key issue is that two ballots of the NUM membership rejected these reforms, and Gormley responded by declaring productivity schemes to now be an issue for the regional committees to decide, with or without a regional ballot. When this was challenged in the high court as a violation of union rules, the court upheld Gormley's decision. This confusion over when the NUM needed to hold a ballot became an issue of huge importance during the 1984-5 strike, when Scargill tried to mimic Gormley's methods and make a national strike into something that regional committees could decide on.

*"He was made a life peer as **Baron Gormley** of Ashton-in-Makerfield in Greater Manchester in the 1982 birthday honours. In 2002 there were allegations that Gormley had worked for Special Branch by passing on information of extremism within his own union. An anonymous witness, who claimed to be a Special Branch officer, made this allegation, saying Gormley did this because 'he loved his country. He was a patriot and he was very wary and worried about the growth of militancy within his own union'."*

Industrial relations discord – who was to blame?

Trevor Bond started as St John's Colliery Manager in 1979. He was originally from Maerdy. Starting in Maerdy Colliery in the Rhondda, via Duffryn Rhondda (closed 1965), Afan Ocean – closed 1968, Glyncorrwg South Pit –closed 1970 and Coegnant Colliery – closed 1981), he had a reputation for preparing pits for closure. Men recall his last days at Glyncorrwg (South Pit) Colliery, when absenteeism was given as the main reason for the pit not being able to survive resulting in closure. This time, in St John's the NUM leadership took up a position for being treated as equals and possessed a strategic approach and a vision of leadership that wasn't going to fall for the old tricks of divide and rule used to prepare the pits for closure. This leadership was younger and prepared to fight for their jobs.

Trevor Bond became manager after Alan Read retired in 1979. In 1980 we, as a lodge representatives attended the funeral of Aneurin Howells former lodge chairman who lived in Alma Road, Maesteg. At the funeral, Alan Read came up to me and said: "If I had known that you were going to stand for lodge secretary I wouldn't have taken you back on the books when you were in college."

I replied that "I knew you wouldn't... so just as well that I didn't tell you my real intentions!" Bond was a mining engineer who thought he could run the pit as his own fiefdom. He would visit the pit unannounced at all times of day and night. He became famous for wearing a neck collar after a car accident and could be seen wearing orange overalls and the white collar.

I established a weekly routine with him where we discussed the affairs of the pit and any disputes and claims by individuals or groups of miners at a Friday morning meeting that would typically last three hours.

There were times when we were at odds over issues, but in the five years I dealt with him, a working relationship was built up where I was able to resolve much of the matters involved in the day-to-day administration and representation of miners, retired miners and widows through negotiations. The overwhelming majority of disputes were settled in house at the pit.

Meanwhile, a lodge official's work goes on

Typical issues dealt with at our weekly meetings with the colliery manager included:

Meetings with the colliery manager:

I.I. CW TMB 17.6.83
12 items to deal with:
Request for down grading to U7 F Stolzenburg 0503 at present a roadman. Request U & prepared to go on the engine, belts etc and continue to do roads if and when asked.
- If he agrees to sign a statement to this effect then agreed.

Dillwyn H Lewis 623 Request for leaving the industry on incapacity - Agree to see NCB doctor.

Tools David Feely, Fitter. Tools on order nearly a complete set pinched in the Bute seam. A note to be provided for replacement.

J Whitlock and others not paid for carrying powder during Whitsun holidays. This has been custom and practice. Manager will look into this with his officials.

May 27, G40 men given the impression by the face Captain Peter Morgan that they could finish early because of their efforts. They were cropped for finishing early and deducted bonus as well.
Manager refused to concede reimbursement – notified him that the matter will be sent for conciliation to the NUM Miners Agent.

Fan men claim for increase in grade from SC2 to S2 – agreed.

II CW TMB 24.6.83
15 items in note book
Request for incapacity D. Bailey following serious accident fracture to tibula and fibula – G40 A load of zinc sheets slid on to his leg causing the injury. Agreed to See NCB doctor.
Islwyn Morris W/E 18/6/83 and 11.6.83 claim for 15ft 5 brings at Cat1, 41ft at Cat 2 remainder 10 rings Cat1. Agreed payment of £31.50 under the incentive scheme.

R Jenkins 265... given light job on booster fan recovering from operation, requests to go back to work on the coalface and not to be downgraded. Agreed to send him to the face to try things out.

23/9/83 4 items to go through with under manager:
H Pye 32... given job on conveyor belt point: request for downgrading – Agreed.

Peter Wooton, temporarily out of place - accommodate until manager comes back – doesn't jeopardise any action the manager may take in this case.
20.9.83 8 men had taxi off afternoon shift – Brewers Bus didn't turn up. Arrived at their homes between 4.50 and 5.10 – agreed payment of shift and reimbursement for taxi
20.9.83 Dayshift G40, six 6 men had to walk out belt on stop. Came up at 2.55pm. Claim for time off or payment made – agreed to await colliery manager return from holidays.

February 1984

Stores: Underwear, balaclavas and donkey jackets needed by men in the pit. None available in the stores. Also Kursey suits needed for G Daniels and E Evans. Agreed to provide what is needed.

D Cadogen and W Sparrow request that in view of their regular attendance that they continue on the books. Manager agreed to look further into this.

G Olphert works underground with ventilation. Request that his rate be regularised at underground rate. He is currently paid S6 Surface rate. He is a second-year apprentice. If he was underground before the holidays he would be paid underground rate. Find out more about what he was doing.

Request answer on G40 improvers upgrading. P Denardy needs further time as improver. Will look at again in a couple of months.

I kept a NUM lodge office at Nantyffyllon Miners Library, open five days a week from 9am to 12.30 pm. I then attended at the pit for afternoon shift on a Wednesday which was docket day. I would return to the lodge office until 5pm or later.

I also went to the pit on Thursday mornings from 6am to 9am to see to the nightshift docket queries and to discuss any pit issues needing resolving with the colliery manager on the following day. I would then be available at the lodge office for the public, members and retired miners and widows.

Typically, the sort of requests we received were for concessionary fuel, membership matters, widows' pensions, and retired miners' pensions.

Men would call in before an afternoon shift to register complaints or to chat over issues that were currently relevant. I would typically then travel to the colliery to meet with the lodge chairman and go over any business. On Wednesday I would be available to answer queries for the afternoon shift and day shift pay dockets. Any unresolved issues would be taken up with the colliery manager as illustrated below: These sessions at the pit were like a surgery with lodge officials and committee men who were available all addressing issues raised by the men and those that filtered through were then addressed by me and or the chairman of the lodge.

17.2.84

1.1. C.W. T.M.B. Meeting between the NUM Lodge Officers and Colliery Manager:

Bus Complaint. Jones' Buses left the pit early, supposed to have taken night shift home 9.2.84. Bus left behind. I Evans and A Trickey, who made their way home after waiting an hour at the pit until 8am. Request travel expenses reimbursed and compensation for one hour's pay. Agreed that manager would pass on the complaint to the Bus company for claim.

Provision of free blocks (men would cut blocks or form bundles out of stick for starting home fires a traditional perk in the mining industry) for workmen). It has been 11 weeks since blocks were available. Request that blocks be made available on a regular basis. Secretary notified colliery manager that he was submitting this matter to the Miners' Agent as the manager was refusing a custom and practice right.

Request that B1 face men be paid 100 per cent bonus for period of working on face when fall in face was holding up face advance.
Refused. This matter would be referred to the Miners' Agent.

It can be seen from the patterns emerging in my notebooks that more reasonable requests for redress of issues were being refused the closer we got to March 5, and the start of the 1984 miners' strike.

Other typical cases taken up from the lodge office included:
Pensions:
NCB, Pensions and Insurance centre
Queens House
Queens St
Sheffield
S1 IGN
Dear Sir/Madam
Re: Mr J Quigley OR 37 42....C, John St Nantyffyllon.
The above ex-miner left the industry in 1969. I would be grateful if you could let me know what pension entitlement is due to him on attaining the age of 65. I am writing on his behalf.

Yours sincerely
Ian Isaac
Lodge Secretary.

Conciliation meetings to resolve issues and disputes.

A conciliation meeting with the miners' agent took place two or three times a year, and included a well-known dispute over snow shifts arising from the

January 1982 snow storm that resulted in as many as 500 disputed shifts for payment for men at the pit who were unable to attend work because of snow drifts and road conditions.

The matter finally went to arbitration whereby, based on a rotation of former NCB officers and two retired NUM officials, there would be arbitration on the case before them. On this occasion, in late 1983, we won the case outright and we congratulated ourselves on fighting a worthy case to the end and won. There was only one outstanding snow shift, that of Bill Pugh, when nearly six months after the award we discovered that his pay number had been mixed up with another and two snow shifts awarded to another miner.

They both ended up being in receipt of two shifts' pay. Such attention to detail was commonplace in resolving disputes.

All change on the committee

By 1982, St John's Lodge Committee had been completely transformed. While retaining some older steadfast committee members, more than three-quarters of the lodge committee, elected through a six-monthly secret ballot at the pithead, were new and younger.

Meetings were also being organised around that time with local activists in Maesteg through the Miners Broad Left. The Labour Party Young Socialists were active in support of the miners, so too were a number of Labour Party members around the left-wing newspaper Militant.

There was a need developing for initiatives around the increase in unemployment in the Maesteg area during the 1970s and 1980s. I was one of the main organisers. There were a few older Labour Party members showing interest in the work at the time including Bill Hayes a close friend of my father and Danny Davies (dogs) who had been a youth organiser for the Communist Party in Duffryn Rhondda Colliery in the 1950s. Others included Jeff Jones and Steve Daniels who were reluctant to join the Labour Party at the time but who participated in the Maesteg Trade Union and Labour Action Committee. Steve was an intelligent participant but reluctant to organise publicly. He joined the Labour Party and latter resigned because of conflict with his career in the Ogwr council - later the Bridgend County Council legal department.

Jeff Jones later joined the Labour Party Maesteg East ward and became a Mid Glamorgan county councillor, when local government was reorganised in 1994 from eight to 22 unitary authorities in Wales. In 1993, ahead of the local government elections he was elected shadow leader of Bridgend County Council, which was to be formed a year later. Most councillors who lived in the Bridgend area were either retiring at the forthcoming new county council elections in May 1994 or had no ambition to become leader. Jeff Jones then automatically became de facto leader of the council until he stepped down in 2006.

A number of us published a local paper through the Action Committee called the Maesteg Pioneer (Keir Hardie's Paper had been the Merthyr Pioneer), which ran to a dozen bi-monthly issues highlighting the plight of unemployment in the valleys. It attracted one or two Labour councillors and others as well as young miners. Through this grouping we continued to organise a number of public meetings in the Maesteg Town Hall in the 1970s and 1980s. Many trade union and Labour Party leaders came to Maesteg at my invitation: Walter Padley MP, Arthur Scargill, Neil Kinnock, George Wright (Regional organiser TGWU and secretary of Wales TUC), Ray Powell local Labour MP, Dafydd Ellis Thomas Plaid Cymru MP, Eric Heffer MP, Dave Nellist, MP for Coventry, and many more. Sometimes the issues were around the campaign against job cuts, no to joining the European Union in the early 1970s, NUM presidential elections and May Day public meetings. Maesteg became politi-cised to an extent that hadn't been seen since the 1920s and 1930s when the miners experienced significant trade union and public political campaigning.

This caused a stir within the Ogmore Labour Party, which made attempts to close it down. Every attempt by the Labour establishment to prevent the activists from campaigning was sidestepped. While the collieries were open, these reactionaries within the Labour Party failed to conduct a witch-hunt to expel supporters of the Broad Left and the Militant newspaper.

These Labour reactionaries only went on to carry out their campaign to expel Labour Party members after the pits were closed and the Miners' Broad Left had been dissipated following the rundown in the mining industry.

Men from other pits transferred in

Following the influx of men from Coegnant Colliery in 1982, by 1983 a number of ex-Coegnant men had stood for election to the lodge committee and Charlie White, a former Coegnant miner, was elected lodge chairman.

Charlie was to become a unique character in the history of the mining industry in the Llynfi Valley. He was of Indian, Gujarati parentage, and brought up in South London. His

Ian and Charlie White, St John's Lodge Chairman

father was a train driver in India who immigrated to Britain after independence. My regard for his approach to trade unionism and life is given later in this book.

This new situation in the coalfield required a new leadership approach at a lodge and area level. We needed to combat the NCB propaganda about uneconomic collieries. The lodge had to adopt a fresh and more engaging approach with its members to keep then regularly informed with research about developments both domestically at pit level and also on an area and coalfield wide basis. This was in order to gain support for the need to campaign against pit closures and the tactics of the Government and the NCB.

Regular election of full-time officials - a principle worth fighting for

At the same time as a general campaign against pit closures we campaigned for internal democracy within the NUM. I had campaigned for the regular election of all trade union officials since the 1970s, when I first became politically conscious after being elected in 1971 at the age of 20 as an AUEW shop steward at the Cowley car works, in Oxford, while working in E Block Paint shop. This was a position I held for nearly three years until I returned to Wales.

I was elected at a time when Lord Soper was chairman of British Leyland. The shop stewards had formed themselves into a combined shop stewards committee covering all the British Leyland plants in England. Derek Robinson (Red Robbo) was chair of the combine committee and the representatives on that body from Cowley were Alan Thornett and Bobby Friar.

Bobby was of Hungarian or Ukranian Jewish descent who was in Vienna when Hitler's troops moved in to annexe Austria. He eventually managed to escape through an emigre network and make his way to Britain.

He settled in the Oxford area and started work at Cowley in 1952. (Source: Alan Thornet, Inside Cowley, 1993). Despite a heavy East European accent he would hold hundreds of shop stewards spell bound at his grasp of the issues confronting the men in the car industry.

I saw him stand on stacked pallets with a megaphone urging men to resist attacks on their working conditions or to call for all-out strike action over a pay demand.

Alan Thornet was a member of the Socialist Labour League (SLL) later to become the Workers Revolutionary Party (WRP). He attended a few meetings of the Miners Broad Left before and during the strike as an observer but made little contribution to the forum, respecting his observer status.

Alan was the architect of the mutuality clause in the Measured Daywork Agreement (MDW) in British Leyland. The shop stewards had negotiated an end to the old piece-work system on the production lines in favour of industrial engineers (time study people) measuring reasonable line speed for men to carry out their various task on production lines.[3]

I had worked on the Maxi production line on the north side of the Cowley plant for a year, and transferred to the E Block paint shop when I returned to work following an accident to my finger on the production line. I was off work for eight weeks at the time.

The mutuality clause of the MDW agreement said that if a man couldn't complete his task in time then help would be given and the industrial engineer (time study officer) and the shop steward would mutually agree the extent of the task required by the production worker. It also stated that if one section of the car plant was on stop because of a dispute in another part of the car plant that men could be paid 80 per cent of their pay for a period of six weeks.

When an industrial engineer walked on to the shop floor without consulting or giving notice to the trade union on E Block to start measuring a man's work, without a shop steward being present to ensure fair play, the whole block of men walked out. The rest of the works were paid while E Block workers were on strike for a fortnight. When they went back to work the management then repeated the provocation by sending an industrial engineer into another department without a shop steward being present. Again, the men walked out for two weeks and everyone else had 80 per cent pay until they returned to work. This went on for three months.

Eventually, with the collusion of the regional officials of the Transport and General Workers' Union, Alan Thornet was sacked by British Leyland despite the fact he was Transport & General Workers Union (T&GWU) deputy convenor of the plant. He had forgotten to update his driving licence and because he was deployed to the part of the plant where drivers drove the finished car off the production line to the car compound, this meant he hadn't complied with the company's regulations.

We went on strike for over a month to try to get Alan's job back, but in the end management stuck to the line that he had not complied with the regulations for his job and they refused to allow him to return to work.

During the three years I was an AUEW shop steward, it was hectic to say the least. I learned more about trade unionism in action in my time at Cowley than in the previous five years after leaving school. I was a shop steward at 20 years of age and had learnt many lessons among older and more experienced men. I also learned not to take anything for granted and to be thorough in the manner that I organised.

I had originally stood for shop steward in the inspection bay where I was transferred to after my accident. I befriended two other inspectors. The notice for nominations was posted and I was proposed and seconded by the two inspectors. Another person also put their name down and I assessed that with 20 inspectors voting that I had a good chance of winning the ballot due to take place two weeks after the nominations.

On the day the E Block T&GWU convenor came around to collect the nomination paper it had been ripped off the board and thrown away.

He declared a new election timetable and a new notice put up for nominations. I again approached what I thought were my two inspector friends and they said sorry but "can't say how, but we can't nominate you this time". They had been got at and I had been outmanoeuvred and discovered that one of the inspectors was a Freemason and he had been told not to support me because of my politics – I was a member of the Labour Party Young Socialists in Oxford at the time.

I put in for a transfer, finding that such clandestine goings on made the working environment weird to say the least. I transferred to the rubbing deck a hundred yards away.

Within three months, I was elected an AUEW Shop Steward for the rubbing deck of E Block - one of two stewards in the block. The two unions - AUEW and TGWU - vied for members throughout the car plant. But the experience served me well. By the time of my nomination for secretary of St John's NUM I was familiar with the need to leave no stone unturned in planning an election campaign within the trade unions.

The AUEW District Secretary, Malcolm Young, an Irish man with pleasant yet intelligent disposition, gave me much support and encouragement - making me the political secretary of the union in Oxford. I headed up the political sub-committee of the AUEW Oxford District for three years before returning to Wales.

My experience at Cowley had by then made me a committed supporter of the regular election of full-time union officials. It was the regional full-time officer of the TGWU that failed to get Alan Thornett's job back. For a first hand account of what took place the reader is referred to Alan's book 'Inside Cowley'.

Stood down as full-time lodge secretary for life

In pursuing the principles of regular election of full-time officers, I arranged to put my position up for regular election. Although I was elected full-time lodge secretary for life in 1978, by 1980 I had given up my right of lifetime tenure of office in favour of a more democratic five-yearly election for the post of secretary. Lodge Full time officers were barred from standing for executive council positions under rule. These rules were a throwback to the days when the miners paid for their own checkweigh-men to check the tonnage of coal coming up the pit to ensure that men received the right pay for the coal they produced. Owners would prevent the checkweighmen from doing their jobs properly [checking the weight/tonnage of lump coal and small coal – only large coal was paid for in those days] so the men would have a levy and pay for their own checkweighmen who would be there to protect the interests of the men.

Ian and other Lodge officials at South Wales NUM Conference, Porthcawl, 1979

The anniversary of the five-year election cycle came up in 1985, after the strike and I was returned unopposed in May 1985.

The St John's Lodge Committee had been to the forefront of a campaign to have all full-time officials of the NUM to be elected every five years - including the national president and general secretary posts. I had demonstrated my commitment to those principles.

The lodge committee had been in favour of this principle from before Thatcher, as prime minister, had brought in legislation requiring trade union officials to be subject to election every five years.

Thatcher had seized upon the perception that the trade union movement was rife with full-time officers who had become a law unto themselves as employees of the unions; safe in their lifetime contracts, a perception which was not far from the truth in the majority of cases. And, unfortunately, many on the left have conveniently forgotten that trade unionism was held back and tarnished in Britain by such practices. It was common practice that these leaders where paid the same as the people they negotiated with, through the TUC policy on parity mentioned earlier, rather than the people they represented.

It was a resolution precisely on the need for five-yearly election of full time officials from St John's Lodge, on which I addressed the NUM conference in 1983. I also proposed, and won the day, at the South Wales NUM conference to have the rules changed - despite sometimes bitter opposition from many South Wales NUM full-time officials. Though it has to be said there was no opposition from South Wales NUM president Emlyn Williams who, I should record, presided over the debate.

It was a notable achievement that by the time the 1984-85 strike started, the national rulebook had been changed to reflect this desire of the rank and file for a more open, democratic leadership in order to fight the battle against pit closures. When I moved the resolution for the election of full-time officials in 1983, at the South Wales Area annual conference in Porthcawl, it failed by only a few votes to get the two-thirds majority necessary for a change of rule. The mood was militant within the coalfield.

Emlyn Jenkins an elected NUM life official as miners' agent for the centre of the South Wales coalfield went to the rostrum at that conference and said: "Over my dead body will this be passed". When I asked for the right of reply as the mover of the resolution, I informed Emlyn Jenkins that while I respected his position, I didn't seek to win this change over his dead body but change will result from this campaign to have officials re elected.

He had no intention of being re-elected or becoming an ordinary miner again even if an agreement was made to guarantee the jobs for those officials who failed to be re-elected.

Their better conditions, their "socialism", had already arrived from within the bosom of the NUM, with higher pay, assisted car purchase and conditions that ordinary miners could only dream about. He wasn't going to give up his status as a permanent NUM full-time official with all its privileges without a fight.

But in the end the campaign of the Miners' Broad Left succeeded. Surprisingly, or perhaps not, those in the Wales Congress and the Communist Party opposed these democratic changes. In the 1983 NUM national conference a resolution was passed allowing for the re-election of officials every five years providing they were less than 55 years of age. The South Wales delegation, after the intervention of Emlyn Williams as president, decided to vote for the resolution in view of the close vote at the South Wales miners' conference. Emlyn had brought wise and expedient council to bear and that's the kind of decision making that marked him out as an exceptionally able president of the South Wales NUM.

I and a few other miners had been instrumental in organising the National Miners' Broad Left since 1979. This body stood in contrast to the NUM official 'National Left' of Arthur Scargill, Mick McGahey, and other national figures, which was organised by Professor Vic Allen from Sheffield University.

Many of those involved in this National Left were the old Communist left - in Wales this involved individuals like Kim Howells, Arfon Evans, the craftsman's rep in Maerdy, and George Rees who was elected general secretary of the South Wales NUM in 1976.

South Wales president, Emlyn Williams, was further to the left as a socialist, than his fellow officers. He had been a Labour Party member and on the Wales Labour

Executive for many years since becoming a miners' agent in the centre of the coalfield.

False starts and dummy runs before the strike

The Tories tried to test out the miners and their relative union strength from time to time with threats of pits closures. If management could get a local lodge to close the pit then the area or national union were powerless to intervene. The Government were also using the opportunity in the early 1980s to prepare for the 'big one', the 'show down', through stockpiling millions of tonnes of coal in power stations (at least a year's supply). They also used the time to headhunt a British Canadian called Ian MacGregor who had earned a reputation during his tenure at British Steel, the nationalised steel industry as it was in the 1980s, for downsizing their labour force and eliminating spare capacity in that nationalised industry. He had been an engineer and a project manager involved in designing the Sherman tank during and after the Second World War.

Determined on a large scale, Macgregor also had a namesake who was chief constable of the British Transport Police in South Wales during the miners' strike. I describe later in the book how this particular Mr Macgregor provided an interesting part to my experience of the strike.

Coegnant Colliery

In 1981, we came out on strike to support neighbouring Coegnant Colliery. The closure announcement by the NCB sparked a coalfield wide strike and was seen by many to be the opening shot in the Tories campaign to close down the British mining industry. It was a sad occasion for Verdun Price, the lodge secretary, who had given his all to keep the pit open. I had built up a good working relationship with Verdun, who never provided an impediment to me campaigning on the issues I was passionate about. He became a friend and mentor during our time together in the NUM, and I always valued his council. Verdun was an extremely competent lodge secretary of independent will and character. It was no accident that he later went on to become a welfare officer for the Coal Industry Welfare Organisation (CISWO) and continued to help many miners, ex-miners and their widows.

As mentioned previously, a new militancy was witnessed at St John's Lodge through the Coegnant miners, and come the time of the 1984 strike many would recall the shabby way that Coegnant Colliery had been treated in 1981. This intake became courageous fighters for the NUM and miners' cause in 1984-85. From the Coegnant Lodge, men like Kinsey Gough, Alan Gould, Peter Derby and Charlie White all developed a strong desire to champion the miners' cause. Tony Cox, a craftsman's rep, together with Colin Day, all contributed to the lively debates on the lodge committee.

But in 1981, after a couple of weeks out on strike in support of Coegnant Colliery, we all went back to work on the recommendation of the NUM. In the meantime, we had set up a 24-hour strike centre, learnt how to organise picket rotas and created a Llynfi Valley strike committee which Verdun headed up. These structures were to be fine tuned by the time of the 1984 strike.

Standing for the NUM South Wales Area Executive Council

In between the two area strikes of 1981 and 1983, in November 1982 I stood for election to the South Wales NUM Executive Council. I took up my post in January 1983 after Verdun Price had stood down.

In the hustings there were two other candidates as well as myself: David Davies (Dai the Red) from Cwm Colliery and David Williams from Wyndham Western Colliery. Tragically, Dai Davies died during the election and it had to be re-run. This time, I had more than five nominations and I was elected by ballot for the second executive council post for the Maesteg district.

In 1983 the South Wales NUM was to go on strike once more against the threatened closure of Ty Mar/Lewis Merthyr colliery. Again the strike lasted two weeks, following which the NCB withdrew their closure list.

At the time South Wales president Emlyn Williams presciently said: "There is no such thing as a copper-bottom guarantee on pit closures. We have not seen the end of this struggle to stop our pits being sacrificed at the altar of Tory ambitions. For now we must go back!" The NCB and the Government had backed off, not yet ready to introduce a massive pit closure programme. They still denied the existence of a closure list that Arthur Scargill had had disclosed from a 'mole' within the Hobart House HQ of the NCB.

Anthony Tynon had become secretary of Ty Mawr/Lewis Merthyr NUM Lodge before the

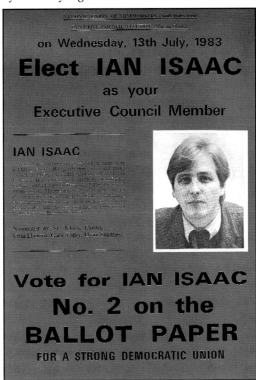

NATIONAL UNION OF MINEWORKERS (South Wales Area)

EXECUTIVE COUNCIL ELECTION (Maesteg District)

on Wednesday, 13th July, 1983

Elect IAN ISAAC

as your

Executive Council Member

IAN ISAAC

Nominated by St. John's, Cordely, Cwm Llynvi, Garw Valley, Llyni Sundries.

Vote for IAN ISAAC
No. 2 on the
BALLOT PAPER

FOR A STRONG DEMOCRATIC UNION

strike. Anthony was a serious and committed young man with militant credentials who was dedicated to his lodge work.

After the pit shut in 1986, Anthony moved in the early 1990s to Maesteg, where he and his wife worked in an old people's residential home. Sadly, he took his own life by hanging in Maesteg near the hospital. Some men tragically could not adjust after the catastrophic collapse of the industry.

At least three other miners I knew in the locality tragically took their lives during that period. The loss of a job in the mines, a way of life, the absence of the comradeship and the dignity that it affords people is a difficult psychological adjustment for all, and regrettably too hard an adjustment for some.

The touch paper is lit

In 1983, South Wales miners' pickets had had a difficult time in the Yorkshire coalfield at the time of the TyMawr/Lewis Merthyr dispute. Although Welsh miners were provided by the Yorkshire NUM with the facility to address pithead canteen meetings the Yorkshire miners at that time had refused to come out on strike in support of their Welsh brothers. Although the NUM leadership in Yorkshire had tried to express support they couldn't take their rank and file with them.

This would be remembered and become a factor in the hesitant start to the 1984-85 miners' strike when the call came from Yorkshire to come out over the announcement of the closure of Cortonwood colliery.

In October 1983, a national overtime ban was imposed. The NUM National Executive Council had the power to call for an overtime ban and have it implemented. So the scene was set for the NCB to make the next move.

1 Margaret Thatcher, Nicholas Ridley Memorial Lecture, November 1996 © Margaret Thatcher Foundation
2 See Andrew Glyn's Pamphlet Keep Mining in Maesteg in appendix.
3 Further reading refer to Alan Thornet's book 'Inside Cowley' 1998 Porcupine press

Maesteg, 1983 May Day march

Most of the men marching took part in the 1984-85 strike. The woman marching in this section behind the banner with the miners was Teresa Parry who was an active member of the Miners' Support Group.

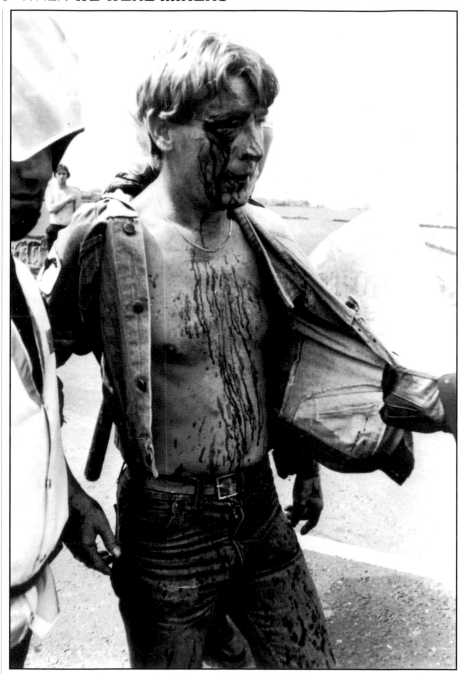

Orgreave

Part two:
The 1984-85 miners' strike

3 Spring: the beginning

EVERY lodge official and rank-and-file miner has his story to tell about the strike. Tens of thousands of miners and their families could give their version of events of the strike and of other times. They all played their part in a common cause for what they saw as not only their future prospects but that of their children and their comrades in the British mining communities. This is my recollection of the events of that great year.

On March 5, 1984, the NCB announced the closure of Cortonwood Colliery in Yorkshire, despite denying previously that it had intended to do so.

South Wales miners - who had had a difficult experience the previous year when visiting the Yorkshire coalfield - argued for us to wait before giving our support.

I understood their reluctance, but the NCB had chosen the time to get this reaction. They were constantly testing the water and trying to goad the NUM into action by announcing pit closures - such as in 1981 over Coegnant, and in 1983 over Ty Mawr/Lewis Merthyr, which were dress rehearsals. This was the real thing.

MacGregor, Thatcher and Marshall and the top police officers were all prepared for the strike. Laws were passed allowing police to stop and search, preventing miners travelling to picket lines and coal was stockpiled in the steel works and power stations.

The NCB had chosen the best time for them to influence any kind of vote or ballot. The manager and his team in my own mine knew what they were doing when they told the men that: "St John's Colliery was safe, don't support those Yorkshire men – they didn't support you."

This interference in NUM affairs by managers was commonplace and designed to influence the outcomes of ballots.

The Yorkshire dimension

During the first week the Yorkshire coalfield was out on strike over Cortonwood Colliery's closure announcement, the South Wales NUM executive recommended at a coalfield-wide special conference in Hopkinstown that "Lodges convene general meetings to support an executive recommendation to come out on strike in support of the Yorkshire coalfield".

St John's Lodge committee met and agreed to endorse this decision and recommended all-out strike action to a mass meeting of the lodge in the Nantyffyllon Institute on Saturday, March 10. With more than 600 attending, the vote produced a majority of 30 not to support the Yorkshire NUM. This was in spite of a vigorous appeal by me and the lodge chairman for solidarity action in support of Cortonwood miners.

I called an emergency St John's Lodge committee meeting later that day. It was a Saturday, and we decided to gauge the mood of the men and investigate why they had narrowly rejected the lodge recommendation for strike action. Lodge committeemen went away to spend the rest of the weekend talking to members on social occasions and in the pubs and clubs to find out why there was such a strong body of opinion against action. We had to understand why we lost the vote.

It had been a long time since the men had turned down a lodge recommendation in a mass meeting. There had to be good reasons for this. The lodge had always prided itself on being open with the membership in arriving at recommendations for action.

We found out that the local management had been busy over the previous few days whipping up discontent with members stating that St John's was not earmarked for closure and that the Yorkshire NUM hadn't supported the South Wales miners the previous year. Some men not in management positions also joined in. There was also a feeling of let them (the Yorkshire miners) show they mean it before we take action in support. Many had also regretted voting against the lodge and having had a day or two to think it over they were ready to vote again.

Picketing at St John's

On Monday, March 12, at 5.30am, a car with four miners from Tower Colliery parked beside the road, underneath the sign that read NCB St John's Colliery. I had been in discussions over the weekend with Tyrone O'Sullivan, and he agreed with me that it would only be necessary to have a small picket presence at St John's Colliery, because I was convinced of the underlying loyalty to trade union principles among the miners at St John's. They would not cross a picket line of another lodge. They hadn't done so three years previously when Coegnant men picketed the colliery.

I made certain that I was present along with the chairman, Charlie White, and addressed the men at the footsteps of the respective buses that came up the pit lane appealing for respect for the pickets and the promise of a further mass meeting as soon as one could be organised to address the current situation in the coalfield. To a man, 350 on the dayshift returned home, the chairman reported the same response from the afternoon and nightshifts.

On the Tuesday morning, March 13, four Tower miners again stood on the side of the road near St John's Colliery, and each car and bus of men allowed the pickets to make their appeal. To a man they only entered the pit surface to collect personal belongings from their pithead baths lockers and then turn around and return home to await further developments. This reoccurred on the afternoon shift and night shifts.

I had, on each occasion, given a dispensation to the colliery manager Trevor Bond to allow a skeleton crew of eight safety men to see to the ventilation and pumping. We had, after all, to have a colliery in working order to return to at the end of this struggle. Throughout the strike I was to maintain weekly contact with the manager over the safety needs of the mine in respect of ventilation, water control and general safety and condition of the mine. We had a list of men on a standby rota to work on safety shifts. All safety men donated the equivalent of a shift's pay per week or 20 per cent of their wages to the strike fund in support of the miners support group.

That afternoon I attended a special meeting of the executive council in Sardis Road, Pontypridd, to assess the situation. The majority of lodges had voted against strike action in support of Cortonwood. This was an embarrassment to the South Wales NUM.

It was reported that pickets from the lodges that had voted for strike action had been out that morning at all the pit entrances and surface installations, and that the vast majority of miners respected the picket lines. Even though some of those who convened mass meetings had lost the vote for strike action - in a de facto sense South Wales was on strike.

The need to re-consult those who had voted against striking

I moved that the EC recommend that lodges who voted against be allowed to reconvene mass meetings in the light of the changing circumstances. Area president, Emlyn Williams, whom I respected greatly, initially argued against this. After some debate, where I was supported by Mike Banwell of Coedely Lodge and Dai Davies from Penrhiwceiber, the president then accepted that lodges be allowed to reconvene mass meetings at their discretion, but that the official position was that the South Wales area would respect picket lines and the decision of the South

Wales NUM was to declare the strike official in the South Wales coalfield. Those lodges who then proved reluctant to retest the mood of their members by convening a lodge general meeting and to decide through a further vote on the new situation (after it had been announced by Phil Weekes Area NCB Director that six pits were to be closed in the South Wales Area) were to experience great difficulty with dissenting members later on in the strike.

Cynheidre Lodge was already experiencing difficulty and it took a number of mass pickets over the following few days to ensure the pit came out on strike.

I didn't underestimate the forces creating instability at Cynheidre Colliery. It was their decision not to reconvene and we respected that decision. The fate of the whole coalfield was at stake and young leaders like Tony Ciano, who I had the utmost respect for, had to make decisions that fitted their particular circumstances as the strike rolled on.

Tony became chair when four of the Cynheirde NUM lodge officials resigned leaving the young leadership pick up the pieces and learn from scratch.

NUM National Rule book: Rule 41

The status of the area was that South Wales was on strike under Rule 41 of the NUM rulebook, which did not specify secret ballots of the membership. The role of the NEC was simply to endorse or otherwise an area that was on strike in support of another area. The general public perceived the NUM to be one union, when in fact it was a number of federated unions each with its own registration with the Registrar of Trade Union and Friendly Societies.

The press and the Government continually attempted to gain some moral high ground over the fact that the NUM had not conducted a national pithead ballot of its members over pit closures, but had allowed areas to determine their own methods of supporting the Yorkshire area under Rule 41 of the national rule book.

The position among the St John's Lodge leadership was that we would campaign for a national secret ballot at the earliest opportunity and would support such a ballot even while on strike. However, the die was cast and we were where we were - a pit on stop with the full endorsement of its NUM members.

NCB confirms a hit list in Wales

Events were gathering pace. On the Tuesday evening, Phillip Weekes NCB Director/Chairman of the South Wales area and a board member of the National Coal Board announced on TV that six collieries would be subject to review for closure and that this included St John's Colliery. The NCB had decided to up the ante to gauge reaction. NCB chairman Ian MacGregor and Prime Minister Margaret Thatcher appeared to have decided that now was the time to create a climate of great uncertainty and insecurity for the future by publishing a list of 24 pits for closure.

On Wednesday, March 14, a reconvened mass meeting took place in Nantyffyllon Institute. Again, more than 650 men turned up. From the platform, I informed the men of the developments since Saturday. The situation had changed. The NCB had been proved to be deceitful over its denials of closure lists. St John's was on it!

We had only one option and that was to fight for our jobs in whatever unity with other miners that we could generate.

When the vote was taken whether to support the decision of the executive to officially declare the South Wales NUM on strike only 20 men voted against. I made the following entry in my diary on the day: *"Reversal of previous decision, 650 at meeting, 20 men voted against."*

That afternoon, following an appeal by the lodge, 480 signed up for picket duty - two-thirds of the membership. A 24-hour strike centre was set up with a rota ensuring a minimum of two men at any one time on duty. Our previous experience of strike action in 1981 and 1983 had taught us to prepare with military precision in order to achieve effective mobilisation of the membership. That evening, 100 men were dispatched by bus to the Nottingham coalfield, which was being heavily picketed by Yorkshire miners.

Pickets were also posted to Shands opencast near Cefn Cribwr in South Wales, and trains were prevented from leaving the site. To the credit of the T&G union members working at Shands no coal left that opencast site during the strike. Teams of six pickets observed the site 24 hours a day, and were witness to the agreement with the workers inside the site. They were allowed to present for work provided there was no movement of coal.

St John's men deployed to play their part

I took a car full of pickets to Ollerton and Thorseby collieries near Mansfield. We knew the area fairly well because the previous year, 1983, we had been guests in the Nottingham coalfield. Charlie White and I had been taken to Calverton Colliery by Roy Lynk, later to become president of the Union of Democratic Miners (UDM).

Lynk, it turned out, was a man with many connections with the state and the media. A former Royal Navy petty officer, Lynk was later to lament in a Sunday Times article that the Tory Government had abandoned the UDM in the 1990s when collieries were closing at a significant rate for uneconomic reasons in the Nottingham coalfield. By then he was president of the UDM, an organisation set up in opposition to the NUM with Government money.

But, in 1982 he was an unelected paid official - finance officer of the Notts NUM. We had been well received by a general meeting of the Calverton miners, who politely listened to our case for unity around the campaign against pit closures. They presented us with a copper engraving of a miner feeding a horse in an underground stable. I kept the engraving (and still have it to this day) because it represents the rank and file and not the UDM leaders.

Nottingham coalfield – the die is cast

Things were to become less cordial in Nottinghamshire over the coming weeks and months.

We arrived in Mansfield at 7pm and met up with pickets from the Yorkshire coalfield. This was in between shifts period and we arranged to come back at about 9.30pm to attempt to speak with nightshift miners arriving for work. There didn't appear to be many arriving for nightshift because most of the coal production took place on the other two shifts.

After a while we drove around the Mansfield area. We then picked up a message on our CB radio that something had happened at Ollerton. We arrived back at the pit about one in the morning to hear that a picket, David Jones from Yorkshire, who had parked his car near where we had been parked earlier, near the back of some houses and a playing field, was seriously ill in hospital.

At the time it was said that someone, in the dark, had thrown a house brick striking him on the head causing serious injury. David Jones, was later to die in hospital through his injuries and become the first victim of the miners' strike. The second victim, Joe Green, was a picket hit and killed by a lorry at a picket line in June at Ferry Bridge power station.

It was the middle of the night and there were by now more than 2,000 men outside the gates of Ollerton Colliery. The Notts NUM president, Henry Richardson, and national president Arthur Scargill addressed the crowd.

It was obvious that some serious thinking had taken place in the previous hour. They both appealed for calm, and in order to prevent any reoccurrence of such a despicable act, Henry Richardson announced that the Notts coalfield would be balloted for an area decision on strike action. Meanwhile, the Notts miners were officially to refrain from work until a pithead ballot early the following week as a mark of respect for the death of David Jones.

In the event, the ballot was 28 per cent in favour of strike with a 68 per cent turnout. Although a defeat, the vote in favour had nearly doubled from 15 per cent in a ballot the previous year on the same issue.

All that remained was that the Notts miners would continue to be picketed with a view to peaceful persuasion. In the event, the tactics of the police were to prove instrumental in inflaming the situation. Many of the miners who voted in favour of strike action came out anyway. Their story is far more heroic than I can tell.

It would be a couple of months before the Notts NUM representing their striking miners (many had come out on strike in the meantime to support the national union) declared the strike official in the Notts area.

By then, the working miners committee with the Chris Butcher, the 'Silver Birch', Roy Lynk, Keith Prendergast and others were virtually members of the UDM in waiting. The working miners committee was later to disown the 'Silver Birch' as a self-seeking publicist.

An example of how the police changed the situation can be described from the experience of St John's pickets. Following the ballot result of the Notts miners, 100 St John's miners were sent to picket the Nottingham coalfield on Sunday, March 18.

By Wednesday, March 21, a further delegation of pickets was sent to Notts. They arrived at Thorseby Colliery in time to picket the afternoon shift only to be confronted by 200 police from the Leicester constabulary.

There were terrific and frightening scenes of police forcing pickets back and not allowing even a six-man picket delegation (allowed under the ACAS code of practice under the Tory Industrial Relations Act) to speak to men when they arrived for work. This lasted for about one hour. I was present for most of the day but made my way back leaving Charlie in overall charge of the pickets.

Organising Picketing at Pontypridd

After this picket, I was called back to Pontypridd to attend a picket co-ordinating meeting at 5pm with Kim Howells, research officer at South Wales HQ. This went on until 11pm. This was the only formal meeting on picketing that I was invited to attend at the Pontypridd HQ.

Although not an elected official, Kim Howells was to play a key role as research officer and picketing organiser in the strike in South Wales as will be described later. Howells had been a part-time research officer appointed because we, the activists in the NUM, had called for a research officer post to keep us informed and help counter the arguments of the NCB in the media and elsewhere.

He had been a part-time lecturer at the South Wales Miners Library in Sketty Road, Swansea, helping Hywel Francis, then also a lecturer, to set up day release courses for NUM lodge committee men through the extra mural department of Swansea University. I had sent four members to the school, all youth reps, from 1978.

In 1982, Don Hayward was taken ill and retired early. Don was a well respected full-time official responsible for pensions and administration in the NUM office. He was an expert stenographer having perfect handwriting and recording skills of writing up delegates speeches at conferences and executive council and other meetings.

Kim Howells became the full-time research officer after Don's retirement. Don's pension and compensation work was then transferred to Cliff Williams, the Assistant Compensation Secretary. Haydn Mathews was by this time in charge of compensation and between them they ended up doing the pension duties.

Kim Howells was a former Communist student activist in the Hornsey College of Art. He never worked underground before becoming a full-time officer for the South Wales NUM.

This would catapult him into the view of the people of Wales. Later in the strike, it would lead to his breakfast meetings with Neil Kinnock the Labour leader, which plotted a behind the scenes "return to work campaign" giving "messages of no hope" to miners on the TV news night after night in January and February 1985.

Later, he joined the Labour Party after many years as a member of the Communist Party. His first attempt after the strike to be selected MP in Caerphilly failed because he hadn't been a member of the Labour Party for at least one year to qualify for nomination. Ron Davies got the nomination and became the Caerphilly MP in 1985.

Howells then became Pontypridd MP in early 1989, after the sitting MP Brynmor John suddenly died in December 1988. Howells was well known in the press and media by then as being the "voice of moderation" alongside Neil Kinnock. The remaining miners' lodges in the Pontypridd constituency nominated him as did the National Union of Railwaymen who always supported the NUM and whose solidarity during the strike was impeccable.

Kim Howells MP is, at the start of 2010, chair of the Parliamentary select Committee on Security and Intelligence but has announced that he will stand down as an MP at the next general election.

Emlyn Williams, suffering ill health, had shown signs of increasing tiredness by the time the 1984-85 dispute had started. He had little time for the constant demands of the media and George Rees, the area general secretary, lacked impact when interviewed on radio or TV.

So, they instructed Kim to become the spokesman for the South Wales NUM. In the strike he was also placed in charge of picketing. Howells had few links with the Maesteg District of the coalfield, except through his informal links with Charlie White, Chairman of St John's NUM. Charlie White was actively encouraged to participate in various fundraising and other projects for Kim Howells during the strike.

Charlie was an articulate activist and we had a bond of loyalty to one another that couldn't be broken by friend or foe. When I was sacked during the strike, Charlie stood by me and even threatened not to return to work after the strike until Ron Roberts, Vic Sedgebeer, Phil White and myself were reinstated. It was only the reassurance of Emlyn Williams that convinced Charlie to return to work and allow the president time to negotiate with area boss Phil Weekes.

Charlie had been invited regularly to help out with welfare and picketing duties at Pontypridd. I never challenged this because I had trust in his overall judgement of where we needed to be in terms of the struggle. The rivalry within the coalfield was between the Broad Left as described earlier and the old Communist Left, which included Kim Howells and George Rees. Charlie found himself between the two but remained neutral, pursuing an independent path.

Certain activities emerge beyond my control

I was one of two executive council members for the Maesteg District that spanned the Afan Valley through to Llantrisant, and covered seven lodges in 1984, but I was never privy to the day-to-day decisions on picketing at the Pontypridd headquarters. I took my instructions directly from the president and participated in the fortnightly executive council meetings which went on as normal throughout the strike.

There were, however, a few dubious requests that came in our direction from the Pontypridd strike HQ for pickets to do strange things. I came back from the Midlands one day to find men in the strike centre making pinholes and blowing the yokes and whites out of eggs and refilling them with paint and then covering over them with sealotape.

These were intended to be thrown at coal lorries leaving the steelworks in Margam.

When this eventually happened, frightening scenes ensued which I told Charlie were out of order and not to be repeated. A similar event took place on the bridge over the motorway at Sarn, near Bridgend, when striking miners from a local valley had colliery hardwoods on the pavement and were about to throw them at lorries on the motorway. The motorway was full of bank holiday traffic.

Fearful of how this could develop, I stopped my car quickly and drove onto the pavement, I told them who I was and asked the men to take the material away and not to be so stupid. This kind of prank could have killed someone.

Such forms of action were not the way of the South Wales miners. Our approach was to think our way through this dispute by appealing for support, raising money for the cause and seeking a platform in the industries that we could get into. We were never going to win by alienating public opinion and by carrying out potentially fatal pranks of this kind.

St Johns men arrested at Thoresby Colliery

One day in April 1984, arriving back at the Nanty Strike HQ, I received a message to say that eight St John's men including the lodge chairman had been arrested and taken to Worksop police cells to appear before Mansfield magistrates the following morning. I had been with them for most of the day and returned to Maesteg when I thought everything was okay. This meant another trip to Mansfield by 9.30am.

A mining colleague and friend of mine for over 35 years, David Hookings, played a prominent part in St John's NUM activities during the strike. He was one of those arrested and recalls how they had been invited by some sympathetic Notts miners to a local workingman's CIU club and enjoyed a meal and a few beers before returning to the picket line for the nightshift.

David Hookings recalls the events leading to his arrest: *"The pickets, about 40 of them, who were in good spirits, decided to march in file (two columns) along the road leading to Thoresby Colliery. This was via a brow in the hill.*

"The police, who were resting in various vans, saw a military-style column coming over the brow of a small hill signing songs and chanting 'left, left, left, left left'. This was a send-up of the normal military chant of left, left, left, right, left. The police must have thought there were hundreds of pickets marching slow over the brow of the hill

some 200 yards from the colliery entrance. There was an almighty scrabble of about 100 policemen who donned their hats and packed their truncheons and riot gear and ran towards the pickets.

"Without a single word being spoken by the police they laid into the miners punching and kicking men who were on the ground having been hit by batons. The end result was over half of the pickets were arrested and dumped into the arriving police vans and carted off to the police cells.

"They were beating me on the floor and Charlie jumped into try to stop the police hitting me, he laid into them saying stop there is enough of you hit me instead lay off him... we were both thrown into the back of police Black Marias"

On the morning of the magistrates court appearance I bumped into a uniformed inspector of the Leicestershire Police at the rear of the court. Ironically, he had all the appearances of a military stereotype himself. He had a handlebar moustache and carried a gilded walking stick, the type that regimental sergeant majors have in the army.

I recall, in some banter, asking why he dressed like this and had he ordered the attack on the pickets the evening before. He wouldn't be drawn.

He wouldn't be drawn again when I inquired why his force was not back in his own county protecting the public from crime, instead of wasting their time creating problems between miners who could sort their own differences out in a much more peaceful fashion if the police were not present!

All eight men were fined £50 for breach of the peace and a further penalty was imposed upon them of being barred from going anywhere within two miles of any pit or power station in the country. In the case of David Hookings he was prevented from picketing at any colliery, steelworks or power station in the country.

This effectively meant that if they were arrested again they could possibly face a prison sentence. The men were all taken off the picketing rota for colliery picketing. We took the decision not to expose the men to further court action and deployed them to fundraising in Birmingham and Plymouth.

Organising the strike 24 hours a day

I returned with the chairman Charlie White to the strike centre. The Nantyffyllon Institute was officially the HQ of the Llynfi Valley Joint Lodges which included the local Washery Lodge and the St John's branch of COSA, the surface officials and clerical section of the NUM.

I was also the secretary of the Joint Lodges Committee in the Llynfi Valley and had convened a meeting to discuss the roles of the various branch officials within it.

A decision was taken that the Washeries NUM Lodge would monitor emergency deliveries of concessionary coal to retired miners and widows. Even though we were on strike we were not going to penalise these people who had either worked most of their lives in the industry or were widows of men who had done the same. All committeemen and many members of the joint lodges were to play a vital role in the organisation of the strike centre in the Nantyfyllon Institute, as will be described later.

The NUM joint lodges in the Llynfi and Afan Valleys was to be in overall control of strike matters. The lodges stood down and only met for domestic matters.

We also formed the Llynfi and Afan Miners' Support Group. It was never called a women's support group. Women and men worked together. Many women's support groups would become independent and seek other remedies for the problems of the area but in the Afan and Llynfi Valleys they remained a loyal and integrated part of the local joint lodges strike committee.

The first two weeks of the strike had been hectic. I went around all our local and national picket sites that St John's men were involved at. These included Parc Slip where the Shands opencast operated. The NUR and ASLEF rail unions had agreed not to transport coal and other minerals from Margam steel works or Shands. This was agreed at a meeting I addressed early on in the strike, in March. Other activities included the placement of caravans at the entrances to the Margam Steelworks and at Shands.

My role was to co-ordinate pickets from the Llynfi Valley, Garw Valley and the Ogmore Valley, which still had a Washery in operation, and the Margam Steelworks. Mike Banwell, the other executive member for the Maesteg District, covered the Cwm and Coedely Collieries and coking works area near Llantrisant.

The Garw, Llynfi Valley, Tondu Workshops, Ogmore Valley and Cwm and Coedely Lodges were all in the Maesteg District, which stretched as far as Church Village near Pontypridd. All these lodges were to be part of a rota of men to man the five gates at the Margam Steelworks during the strike.

At different times during the strike there were some unusual as well as heavy scenes on those picket lines outside the steelworks.

Picketing at Margam Steelworks

British Telecom workers respected the picket line and turned back and so did many hauliers. I recall one occasion when a French lorry driver turned up at the main gate at the eastern end of the steel works. Pickets, myself included, stepped out in front of the lorry with placards and gestured for him to stop. He did. When I approached the drivers cab and began to speak to him, he uttered something like "non anglaise" I signalled in a circle with my index finger for him to turn back and he shrugged his shoulders and pointed as if to gesture to turn around. He went in to the works to turn around. I reflected later that picketing was an international language!

When he turned around on the traffic island there was a great cheer from about 100 miners who were stood on the grassed area at the side of the road.

Early on in the strike it became apparent that mass picketing on its own could not be the only strategy and there was a need to develop mass support for the NUM. We responded to numerous requests to speak across the country. I couldn't do it all myself and a sensible rota was drawn up and we would meet to decide who would address what meetings. The committee would start to develop their speaking skills.

How pickets were deployed

Written instructions were typed up for every group of pickets and every driver as in this example: *"Whitwick Colliery (Leicester Area) Maesteg M4, A449/M50 then on to M6 go south to Junction 2 take M69 to Leicester. A46 to city centre on to inner ring road till reach Blackbird Road past Blackbird pub across Junc. sharp right bend to parker drive (you'll pass the Marconi factory) at the end of Parker drive turn left again into Halifax Drive. Ask for Stocking farm Est. Accommodation arrangements have been made with Steve S (xx) Hipwell Crescent. Stocking Farm Est. Leicester Tel: 0533 -35... This will be your destination for the night.*

Steve S will then give you arrangements for digs and the best route to the pit etc.

When you get to the pit try to contact the local Officials and distribute leaflets. Don't dump them in the canteen try to hand them out personally. Combine Picketing with making contacts with local miners and if possible local NUM branch officials.....Ring back reports daily".

We also had requests from the wider movement including university students.

Typical was the following example:

Requests for speakers: May 1984

Letter From Heiko Khoo, secretary Portsmouth NUS, requesting Ian to speak at their rally in support of an occupation of halls... We thank you for the support you gave us at the beginning of our action, which was received with cheers from the students. Agreed to send Bobby Potts St John's Committeeman to speak on behalf of the Lodge in view of his close links with the NUS in that area.

Reaching out to the wider movement

Appealing to the wider trade union movement, especially those reliant on coal or those in control of key stocks of material and fuel for the electricity generating industry, required a fresh, often innovative approach. The memory of the generating crisis and three-day week rationing fuel in British industry in 1974 was still fresh in the minds of the activists.

Miners appeared on BBC2's Newsnight', the news and current affairs programmes in numbers never imagined before the dispute began. It was like a

Caerau women campaigning

genie was let out of the bottle. Such latent talent for leadership and such uncondi-
tional support from so many was a revelation. That was why we felt on the cusp of
victory so many times during the strike. We kept the campaign for our case up there
in the forefront of the news, the trade Union movement, the Labour Party and via
every conceivable social gathering during those hectic months.

As an executive council member, I urged the South Wales NUM president to meet
with the steelworkers union at the Margam plant. I arranged this meeting during
April.

I attended along with the area officials, vice-president Terry Thomas, Emlyn
Williams and George Rees, and met with the steelworkers' leaders in an effort to get
an agreement that would avoid the need for heavy picketing at the steel works gates.

The meeting with steelworkers' unions - men from ISTC, NUB - also included
reps from the rail unions ASLEF and NUR, and went ahead after I had made
approaches to their respective unions on behalf of the leadership.

Emlyn Williams had a good reputation for negotiation and clear thinking in such
situations. He urged the steelmen to refuse to handle coal including the offloading
of coal from the harbour. The NUR and ASLEF reiterated their commitment not to
transport any coal by rail to Llanwern Steelworks, which was fed daily with coal
from Margam. The steelmen explained their dilemma having undergone a massive
"slimline" as they called it (a reduction of manpower through redundancy) in their
operations when Ian Macgregor, now chairman of the NCB, was chairman of
British Steel.

Our relationships with the steelmen had been good since their three-month strike in 1982. We had campaigned since 1979 alongside unions such as the steelmen to fight to protect jobs as well as wages. In the event the ISTC leader Bill Sirs signed an agreement in 1982 which dealt with the wages issue only and had no guarantees for jobs. "We'll settle the pay dispute first", he said, "and deal with jobs later". The die was cast. The steelmen had seen 20,000 jobs disappear in the previous two years and were weary of strident industrial action. However, at the meeting they agreed to do what they could to support the miners.

They set up fundraising initiatives and the majority of steelworkers donated a regular amount for the duration of strike to support the NUM. Many also gave individual donations to pickets on a daily basis. The money was then handed on to help with assistance in the various miners support funds for food parcels and help with hardship.

However, while the meeting maintained goodwill between miners and steelworkers, it didn't result in a programme of progressively shutting the works down to bring pressure on the government to concede to the miners demands for a veto on pit closures unless through proven exhaustion of reserves at coal mines.

N.U.M. South Wales Area

APPEAL to MARGAM STEELMEN

MINEWORKERS in South Wales are organising

A MARCH AND RALLY

IN PORT TALBOT—11.30 a.m.
THIS FRIDAY, 20th APRIL

It will draw the attention of all working people in Port Talbot and Wales to the issues facing the N.U.M. in ITS FIGHT TO RETAIN MINING IN SOUTH WALES.

You can help by attending the March and Rally; by encouraging your workmates at your place of work the need to COME TO THE AID OF THE MINERS!; by agreeing to restrict the importation of Coal and stopping Coke leaving your Plant!

The B.S.C. would use Port Talbot Steel Works to undermine the effect of the Miners' Strike! You have more in common with the Miners than you do with B.S.C. Bosses!

OUR FUTURE IS YOUR FUTURE

Refuse to offload Imported Coal from Foreign Vessels; STOP COKE LEAVING YOUR PLANT;

JOIN OUR MARCH — SUPPORT THE N.U.M.

If you want to help the N.U.M. — please contact 0443 - 404092 or Maesteg 739151 or Llangeinor 870084

COAL NOT DOLE

Published by N.U.M.
and printed by Gibbs, Printers, Maesteg.

NUR and ASLEF - rail workers stand firm

It would be true to say that the only section of the trade union and Labour movement who instinctively understood the miners' dilemma were the railworkers. This affinity had echoes of the past, of the Triple Alliance of miners, transport workers and railwaymen during the 1926 general strike. More recently, rail workers had lost thousands of jobs unnecessarily during the 1950s and 1960s.

Such consciousness transcends generations.

We received exceptional support from the NUR and ASLEF. Everywhere I went, if I met a rail worker their support was without qualification. I spoke on more than one occasion at the rail workers' club in Port Talbot as a guest of the rail unions.

In the executive council meeting of June 29, 984, (where I was present) Minute 339 refers to: *"Ian Isaac suggested that thanks should be made for the tremendous support given to the NUM during the past weeks by the Rail Unions... It was resolved to place official thanks to the NUR and ASLEF in the minutes."* Why not by letter I don't know, but there are times when you accept a record of appreciation like crumbs from a table.

Picketing at Margam steelworks was to be a permanent feature throughout the strike and events in the steelworks would flare-up from time as British steel adopted tactics to get around the stranglehold of the picket lines and the rock solid boycott imposed by NUR and ASLEF.

Coal convoys - Margam to Llanwern

Road convoys transporting imported coal from the Port Talbot docks to the Llanwern Steel works were being organised to keep the production of steel going.

Read Brothers Transport, based in the Forest of Dean, was the first to provide convoys of lorries to take coke from Margam Steelworks to Llanwern Steelworks some 50 miles east along the M4. These strike-breaking companies made millions of pounds profit from this kind of bounty money to help break the miners stranglehold on the steel and power industries.

Throughout the strike NUR and ASLEF never allowed one lump of coal to be transported by rail despite threats to their own jobs.

In response to the increasing numbers of lorries in convoys coming out of Margam heading for Llanwern, the number of pickets was increased. It was clear that many lorries were not roadworthy and lacked proper documentation. They were never stopped or checked by police. Perhaps they were subject to a sealed corridor as a police no-go area of operation.

One morning in May, the police massed in bigger numbers than normal, so men came from other gates and from the local lodges to demonstrate our disapproval at this escalation in coal traffic.

Injured picket outside Margam Steelworks

At the Margam Number 5 gate, near some houses that had their own inner road, two police constables were hitting a small young miner with batons - having held him over the bonnet of a car. My first instinct was to jump on one of the cops and restrain him from hitting the young man. Others must have joined in. The next thing I can remember is being carted off and bundled into a Black Maria by six constables, one on each arm, one on each leg and two grabbing my clothing at the side.

I was taken at 10am to Port Talbot Police Station. We were put eight to a cell. Eight bewildered pickets in a police cell with wooden benches and the only other facility being a toilet with a half screen by it. We were offered a plain white bread ham sandwich in the afternoon with a cup of tea. By the end of the afternoon all the pickets were processed and I was left on my own in the cell.

I kept inquiring when I would be charged and released but nothing happened. Suddenly, at 9pm, I was taken to the duty sergeant's desk told to sign a form, my personal effects returned to me including a little bit of money I had carried and I was then released. I phoned home for my father to pick me up.

A month later we appeared at Port Talbot Magistrates Court and were all found guilty of breach of the peace and fined £50, with a further stipulation that we were not to go within a mile of a steelworks, power station or coal stockpile in the country.

Court appeal

I decided to lodge an appeal against my conviction to act as a benchmark for others. It turned out that my barrister, a Mr Lloyd Lloyd who represented me at Swansea Crown Court, had gone over the papers and felt able to present a case of wrongful arrest as part of the defence appeal.

I presented him with a reel of photos which had been taken on the day by pit electrician Paul Davies (Davis). We had organised for Valley and Vale photographers - a community arts project - to accompany us on all public events during the strike. They have a vast collection of strike memorabilia and images to this day in their Garw Valley premises. I turned up in court wearing the same clothing that I had worn on the day of the arrest. A photo showing my arrest by six policemen was displayed and I could recognise it was me because of the sole of my left shoe and the colouring of my short sleeve jumper and shirt.

I took my shoe off in court and it was handed to the judge who inquired if this was the right shoe. "No your honour, it's the left shoe", said the barrister. "Is it the right left shoe?" replied the judge with a sense of humour that lightened up that part of the proceedings.

Two police officers were then called as witnesses by the prosecution lawyer.

When they appeared in the witness box it suddenly occurred to me that I not seen these men before in my life. They said, reading from their note books that the accused was "gestulating" [sic] (I had never heard such a word before) with his arms in the air and shouting: "Get stuck into them boys", again a phrase I had never used before in my life let alone "gestulating" in the air with my arms!

I later assumed they meant gesticulating.

My barrister cross examined them and asked to see their notebooks for the day in question. It turned out there was no reference to arresting anyone at 10am in the morning - their first arrests were at 11.15am on the morning in question. It also turned out that they couldn't recognise who was who from our photograph which showed all six faces of the arresting officers.

These hapless police witnesses had not been the arresting officers and the charge sheets had been falsified. The judge interjected: "It appears that someone in this trial may be committing perjury". Myself and a group of about 12 miners attending in the public gallery were pointing in unison to the police officers in the witness stand and we all said together: "Yes, it's them".

The judge dismissed the court and the appeal was upheld. Hundreds of miners had been arrested and fined and bound over to keep the peace. My stand was a small contribution to demonstrate that most arrests were based on the spurious and false charges in circumstances staged and engineered by the police.

Touring the coalfields as executive council member

The period from March to June was to prove a consolidation of organisation. I travelled to places like Rufford Colliery to address groups of South Midlands' miners and miners in other areas on the situation in South Wales.

I was at Daw Mill Colliery to make an agreement with a regional T&G union official that T&G drivers would not deliver oxygen to the pit which experienced "Outbursts" in the hope that the colliery would be declared unsafe for production. A safety crew would be allowed to work but no production I hoped.

It resulted in the lorries coming down the pit lane with the drivers jumping out 200 yards from the pit and leaving the keys in the lorries. Working miners then came out of the pit and drove the lorries in. Not all the men agreed to drive the lorries in and soon there was a queue of lorries a mile long back up the pit lane.

I finally agreed to allow the recommencement of deliveries on the advice of the NUM national safety officer. The strike was sometimes all about small victories and attempts to prevent coal being produced. More than one imaginative idea or devise was used.

Mobilising public support

An invitation by Liverpool Students Union for me to engage in debate with the NCB industrial relations officer resulted in a massive yes vote in support of the

NUM, which was reported in the Liverpool Echo as further evidence of the popular public support for the miners' strike.

"Miners win the pits battle... at university"

Proclaimed an article by Alf Bennett of the Liverpool Echo on Friday, October 12, 1984. *"The National Union of Mineworkers won its bitter eight-month strike battle – but that doesn't mean the men will be back at the pits. Their victory came, not in national talks, but in a war of words at Liverpool University's Students' Union... the debating society staged the pits confrontation in miniature... The NUM took on officials of the Coal Board and a solicitor representing working miners in the Stanley theatre – and won...*

"The motion: 'This house would dig deep for the striking miners' was won by an overwhelming majority but not until fiery words had been exchanged...

"Ian Isaac, an executive member of the South Wales NUM told students: 'Either we win this battle or we will be relegated to the dustbin of the dole queue'. He said the dispute is not about economics – given the cash lost in halted production and the extra money paid out for policing – but a political effort to destroy the miners' union. The authorities recognise the miners' union as the brigade of guards of the trade union movement...many trade unionists now recognise that if the miners lose then they lose as well.

"Alex Jeavons of the NCB's Western industrial relations department said: 'For us in the NCB the dispute is not about politics, nor is it about a tough sheriff brought in to deal with Billy the Kid . . . the plan for coal recognised that some pits would close once their useful economic reserves of coal are depleted'.

"Mr David Megus, solicitor for the National Miners Committee said: 'My clients are all union loyalists and while they continue to work they are not by and large in favour of pit closures – that would be rather like turkeys favouring an early Christmas...the problem has arisen in this dispute is that people haven't been given a vote'."

The article concluded by stating: "One practical measure which emerged yesterday was that students are to set up a miners support group at the university."

Amongst numerous speaking engagements was an Anti-Apartheid rally I addressed in Swansea, which again endorsed the struggle of the NUM. Another speaking engagement was a speech I gave to the Northumberland and County Durham Miners and their support group in Newcastle City Hall. It was a fundraising event with the local folk and pop group Lindisfarne. A photo of me in front of the drum kit and guitars was put up in our strike centre and stayed there for the rest of strike. Some wag had printed in pen in speech bubble pasted on to the photo: "The fog on the Tyne is all mine comrades!" There were moments of humour and pathos as well as committed organising during the strike"

The special conference and the national ballot

On April 12, the NUM executive met and voted to place a number of resolutions on the future course of the strike to a special conference in Sheffield on April 19, and in the meantime endorsed the areas on strike as being official under Rule 41. I was of the opinion even then that a decision should be taken at a conference with a view to conducting a national ballot while on strike. At the special conference a massive demonstration of miners from every part of the coalfield was in attendance lobbying delegates as they entered.

The intensity of opinion among miners' ranks was mixed. Those who believed that the strike was the only stand the NUM could take against pit closure were concerned that the establishment were gathering public opinion in favour of a national ballot through accusing Arthur Scargill and the NEC of being undemocratic, and that this could be used to influence rank-and-file opinion resulting in a vote against strike action on pit closures. Many felt that the NCB had started the action and those on strike had a right to strike without a national ballot under each respective area's leadership and each area rule book. A combination of miners being picketed out with areas endorsing the action and area ballots was the mixed consensus in the early days of the strike.

Eventually, the special conference voted for the Kent resolution which was a composite motion. In effect this meant that the conference declared the strike official without a national ballot under Rule 41.

Events had now reached such a pitch that there was no going back. However, the fact that no national pithead ballot was called would allow the Government and the establishment to provide constant and irritating reminders that the rank-and-file miner couldn't be turned on and off like a tap over pit closures by either the state or their union. While the majority of NUM members were on strike for the duration of the strike, there was however a significant majority of Notts. and South Derbyshire miners, who were to report for work passing through the picket lines with police escorts throughout the strike.

History would suggest that on previous occasions when there was a national ballot in 1972 and 1974 that a small majority in favour of strike action was sufficient to generate 100 per cent unity in the ranks. I recall when meeting miners from Nottingham, picketing at the Cowley Car works in 1972, that while some miners then voted Conservative at general elections; they were either totally or passively committed to the strike which lasted eight weeks.

In 1974, the majority in favour of further strike action was even higher. It had built on the success of the previous action. The 1974 action was to lead to the downfall of the Heath Tory Government and restore the miners' relative position in the unofficial industrial workers pay league.

Sometimes a national ballot can create and legitimise strike action; other times it can bury it, resulting in handing the initiative to the management. The Government knew that and had picked their moment to provoke strike action in the hope that a ballot would vote down action.

The strike had begun because the NCB announced pit closures in Yorkshire and other areas such as Wales a week later. Those areas which had pits earmarked for closure were solidly out on strike. But, it had been a tactic of the NCB not to announce closures in the Nottinghamshire, South Derby or Staffordshire coalfields. Nor did they announce any pit closures in North Wales.

It makes interesting reading to see what the press were saying in the 1972 strike when a national ballot was held and a decision taken for strike action, when there were still headlines such as "Miners holding the country to ransom" and "Miners can't win".[1]

The matter was settled. Such was the intensity of the thousands of miners lobbying the conference that April day, combined with the fact that 90 per cent of the British coalfield had voted with their feet, and the question of a national ballot would be relegated to the ivory towers of the newspaper editors and those politicians seeking constitutional sanctuary for the actions of miners attempting to save their industry. The debate was over as far as the miners at the time were concerned.

However, even to this day the question of what would have happened if miners had held a national ballot while on strike is being debated!

"If 'ifs' and 'ands' were pots and pans there would be no debates for politicians." (I have adapted an old saying my grandmother used to say).

The reality is who knows what the outcome would have been. We know what outcome Margaret Thatcher, Ian MacGregor, Nicholas Ridley, the nuclear power lobby and the right wing of the Labour movement wanted – an end to coalmining in Wales and the rest of the UK bar for a few super pits to supply the power stations.

Yet, if a national ballot had been held on strike action in April 1984, it was odds on that a majority would have voted in favour. Although a vote in favour would certainly not have stopped M15 and the special branch. The Prime Minster's office would not have abandoned their dirty work creating an alternative union in the Midlands and elsewhere in the shape of the UDM. There seems little doubt 25 years on that some leaders of the Midlands Miners were in the pay of the state and participated in its covert operations. They wouldn't have recognised the legitimacy of a majority vote in favour of strike action in a national ballot, whatever the circumstances. This was make or break for both sides and it was as much a challenge to the TUC and the Labour Party as it was to the NUM.

Doing my duty locally

In April 1984 I concluded a no-movement of coal agreement with Mr Richard Crookes, general manager of South Wales Wharfage Ltd in Briton Ferry. This was a small coal distribution depot for the distribution of coal offloaded at the wharf from ships able carry up to a thousand tonnes of coal.

This released up to 16 men who would have picketed this site around the clock. Instead, only one person from time to time would observe the site to see that the agreement was intact. It remained intact throughout the strike for nearly a year. I never did get the chance to follow this up with an expression of thanks to Mr Crookes. I hope this gesture of referring to him in this account goes some way towards the recognition he deserved for having the foresight to retain some social and political dignity in not moving his not to inconsiderable 50, thousand tonnes of imported coal during the strike.

In May I concluded an agreement with the TGWU over Berkley A and B nuclear power stations, limiting the supplies of oils and oxygen. This remained in place for many months until it too was handed over to the national NUM safety officer.

Doing my duty in the Midlands

In the early months of the strike St John's men became established in Birmingham. We had a picketing presence in the North Staffs coalfield for a few months. The following is an account of my visits to Birmingham and the welcome we were given wherever we went:

We had previously given written typed instructions to all car drivers going to Picket Daw Mill Colliery (Warwickshire):

'Destination Daw Mill Colliery (Warwickshire)
Maesteg M4 to Newport Area M50 turn to Monmouth towards Birmingham M5 Junction 1 A41 to Birmingham to A34 (on the way you pass West Brom Football

ground and on A34 go down Holyhead Road, Soho Road – take signs for Hockley turn left down into Hockley into Icknield Street – you will see the Mohammad Ali Centre on your left on the left hand side of a one way road.

The man in charge of the centre is a West Midlands County Councilor James Hunte. That will be your base. Dawmill mainly coals on days and nights. Day shift 7pm nightshift 10.30pm. A small preparation shift goes in on afternoons between 12.30 and 1.30pm.

The pit is three-hour traveling time from the base. The best way to get there to start with is to get out of Birmingham City Centre to M6 motorway south to junction 5 go to Coleshill ...through Coleshill to a village called Shustoke. Keep going until you get to Furnace End in which case you either get through it or walk 1 ½ miles to the pit.

The pit is 20 years old and has a life of 45 years with over a million tonnes a year output. When there try liaise with Kent Miners at AUEW/Tass 6 Holloway Circus Queensway, Birmingham 1 021-632-4551.

Also try to contact local Lodge officials and find a good way of distributing the leaflets. It is no good just leaving them in the canteen. They should be handed out personally if possible.

Mohammad Ali Centre 021 554 – 9055.

Ring back reports daily.

Mohammed Ali Centre, Handsworth.

In the late spring of 1984 when we were picketing Daw Mill, Baddesly, Birch Coppice and Coventry collieries in the North Staffs coalfield, we were the guest of James Hunte a local Birmingham city councillor who made significant resources available to support pickets during the strike.

Handsworth was a centre for African-Caribbean immigrants many of whom were second generation. James himself was a descendent of slaves adopting the name Hunte with an "e" on the end, which he informed me denoted that he originated from slaves in the Caribbean as distinct from the slave owner who would have spelt his name without an "e".

He was a fascinating character and organised for over 50 pickets at a time to billet at the local Mohammed Ali Community Centre. They slept on the judo mats and showered in the facilities made available to them. Many miners were encountering a large ethnic minority population for the first time and were bowled over by the hospitality. Any prejudices they may have harbored melted away in the warmth of the support provided for them. Picketing duty normally started at 5am with a 40-minute journey to the pits.

On one occasion, when I was there negotiating with the Transport & General Workers Union (T&G) over movements of oxygen lorries, a number of men went out to a local night club. They were still not back at the centre by 3am. So a local caretaker of the centre went out searching for them. He found them okay and provided an escort back to the centre for a couple of hours of much-needed sleep before going on the picket line.

I was accompanied on this visit by Vic Sedgebeer, the COSA secretary from St John's, who I was keen to involve in the dispute as much as possible. Miners in the main, white collar ones included, respected their leaders and it was no exception for Vic. If Vic was on side then his members were.

Meeting Mohammed Ali

To our surprise, James Hunte called in to announce that Mohammed Ali, the great heavyweight world boxing champion was going to visit the centre to sanction its naming after him. James gave an invitation to have lunch with himself and his family to myself and Vic - to be seated each side of the great boxer himself.

I recall that he was tall and slim and wore a black tunic-type suit with a smart black open neck shirt. His movements were slow and deliberate and carried out with much poise and style. It was later that I discovered that he was suffering with the early symptoms of Parkinson's disease, no doubt brought on by his heroic battles in the ring. He had retired only three years earlier after his last fight - a non-title fight with Trevor Berbick. That was 10 years after his "Thrilla in Manilla" with Joe Frazier, where he fought in 100 degree heat. Ali won when Frazier failed to come out for the 15th and final round.

I tried my best to hold a conversation with him about the miners' strike. I said the British miners were great fans of his and that I had been a fan since he beat Henry Cooper in that controversial fight in 1963 and then Floyd Patterson in 1965. I asked his secretary, a stern and serious, but courteous, individual, if she would take a letter from me for Mohammed to give a donation to the striking British miners.

The copy in my papers reads:

Mr. Mohammad Ali, At the Community Centre, Birmingham, England
5-5-'84

Dear Mohammad,
The bearer of this letter represents the South Wales miners who have been using the community centre during the Miners' dispute with the kind permission of Mr. James Hunte and his colleagues.

As a token of our gratitude we are presenting Mr. Hunte and your good self with a miner's safety lamp.

We realise the tremendous amount of work that you do throughout the world for working people and wish it to be noted that many miners are fans of yours and have a keen interest in boxing and other matters.

At present we are in the eighth week of strike trying to stop pit closures and 60,000 job losses over the next three years. It could be a long and bitter struggle. If in some small way you could mention the plight of the British mineworkers when you get home it would be appreciated.

Also, if at all possible, if there are any trusts or charities that would be inclined to help us financially then it would be most welcome. Miners support groups have been set up in the communities and are providing food parcels for single miners who get no money and also families where wives aren't working only get about £10 per week to live on. We have mentioned this in case there may be a little help over in America. Trusting your stay in Britain will be enjoyable and happy.

Yours sincerely, Ian Isaac Executive Council NUM (S Wales Area)

It wasn't exactly a demanding type of letter and I didn't get a reply, but then I wasn't holding my breath. Perhaps he didn't want to be seen to alienate any of his fans who happened to be opposed to the strike. You never know there may have been some!

In the evening we were entertained in the centre to a fabulous buffet and live African dancers and singers. Fifty miners from the Llynfi and Afan valleys and 200 local people from Handsworth with Mohammed Ali sat centre stage surrounded by young people and children. He remained dignified while I was invited to present him with a gift from of a Miners Davy Safety Lamp. Terry Furlong, whose wife Eirlys was an active volunteer in the miners' support group back home in the Llynfi Valley, recalls the occasion well. Every time I bump into Terry he reminds me of that occasion. The evening passed off well and then it was time to pack away every bit of equipment and get out the gym mats to rest on before another early morning picket.

Before I left to go home to Maesteg, James Hunte gave us all a civic reception at Birmingham City Hall. For us it was like having the freedom of the city. They had done so much for us.

Picketing out of Birmingham

Mary Colyer, an official of Nuneaton and District Trades Council produced a 10,000-word personal account of the Miners strike called **The Birmingham Occupation.**

The following extract refers to an incident at Daw Mill Colliery in the Warwickshire Coalfield.

"DAW MILL – BOC (British Oxygen Corporation)
"Pickets at Daw Mill reported that BOC lorries were delivering twice a day, a

consignment of liquid nitrogen. Inquiries were made why such deliveries were being made; it was found that these supplies of liquid nitrogen were essential to control the heating in a coal seam at the pit. If deliveries were stopped, it would mean that for safety, no-one would be able to work underground.

"I contacted South Wales NUM and gave them the information and asked for guidance, as the BOC drivers (TGWU members) did not want to cross the picket lines, some did not, they were instructed to leave the lorry at the gates with the keys in the ignition. NCB drivers then came out and drove the lorries into the pit. The drivers felt that if their union and workplace was officially approached by the NUM, then some sort of agreement could be made with the NCB. It was suggested that a meeting be arranged with TGWU district secretary and conveners at BOC Wolverhampton, from where the liquid nitrogen was been sent to Daw Mill. Problems were still being experienced in not having a representative from South Wales based in Birmingham on a regular basis.

"I explained to 'Ponty' office that a meeting could be arranged, but it would be helpful if an EC member was available, as it would carry more weight when discussions with T.G.W.U took place.

"An EC member was sent, this being Ian Isaac from St John's, Maesteg. Ian arrived on May 8, and after I had explained the situation to him, he telephoned the TGWU district secretary and explained the situation to him the following afternoon. Geoff Poxon, a NUPE official, went with Ian to meet H Littlehales TGWU district secretary. It was explained to him what the situation was at Daw Mill. Littlehales agreed to recommend with his shop stewards for the drivers to adhere to the picket lines, as for the drivers leaving the keys in the cabs, Littlehales agreed to have this stopped.

"Ian Isaac and Geoff Poxon returned back to Birmingham to await the outcome of the meeting that the TGWU had arranged with BOC management later that day.

"Littlehales phoned through the next morning at 9.35am to say that the NCB had been notified that as from Sunday (13.05.84) ALL supplies of liquid nitrogen would cease. They had been given three days' notice for safety requirements to be met; they also agreed to re-establish deliveries when all miners working at Daw Mill had been laid off. Out of a workforce of 1,350, only 26 were on strike.

"While in Birmingham, Ian Isaac reviewed the situation in the area and made out a report for South Wales, the following are extracts from that report:

"Midlands NUM (Warwickshire – Cannock – North Staffs)

Nitrogen or Daw Mill comes from BOC Wolverhampton. H. Littlehales TGWU secretary for B.O.C has instructed members not to leave keys in cabs for N.C.B drivers to take nitrogen in. This has been dealt with. Also no oxygen going directly from BOC into Anseley Workshops. National N.U.M should be informed to see if agreement can be made for pit to be out before dealing with safety problems.

Suggestions to Pontypridd:
1. *That COSA men be sent up for picket to picket out COSA men at pits.*
2. *That pickets stay until Friday teatime, because lorries going in Friday afternoon.*
3. *Dordon Nr. Tamworth – ex Scots and Geordie miners live in village and work at Daw Mill. See if Scots and Geordie miners can be sent down.*

No's Out	Pit in Warwickshire	No. of Men
26	Daw Mill	1,350
9	Baddesley	1,046
60	Birch Coppice	836
90%	Coventry	1,400
5	Anseley Workshop	280

Key pits for mass picketing – Daw Mill, Littleton, Hem Heath.

"This report was sent to South Wales NUM. Ian Isaac was recalled to South Wales and further developments with the liquid nitrogen fell through. They never did stop deliveries. Everything went wrong and it was rumored among the South Wales lads that Ponty had called it off because of the danger of the pit closing down altogether. A 24-hour picket was kept on Daw Mill for a further three months, but this was wasted manpower as the BOC drivers continued to cross picket lines."

It was, in fact, called off because of the advice of the national NUM safety officer. The aim of the NUM wasn't to create so much damage that a pit would be closed through lack of safety. I agreed with the decision and abided by the advice. The aim was to encourage the miners to come out on strike and to ensure that safety teams were provided to keep the mines clear of harmful gases, well ventilated and safe for when the strike was over. We wanted well maintained pits to return to.

1 (A quote from an article written by Idwal Isaac and a Labour Research pamphlet, Volume 61 No.4 April 1972.)

4 Heading for summer: the strike gets serious

Orgreave - the trap

n May I concluded the first of two agreements with the T&GWU over Berkeley A and B nuclear power stations limiting the supplies of oil and oxygen. This remained in force for a few weeks until it was handed to the jurisdiction of the NUM national safety officer. There were a lot of controversial decisions made at this time. Billy Hyde, who was secretary of Bedwas NUM Lodge states that he was handed documents signed off in the name of George Rees, general secretary South Wales NUM, giving dispensations to nuclear power stations.

Whether these were forgeries or some kind of state sleight of hand interventions we shall perhaps never know, but it had the effect of allowing nuclear power stations to continue their base-load operations. (Power distribution within the UK is based on a base-loading system whereby nuclear power stations run continuously and coal fired stations are run to add to the base load to meet peak demand – this is the most economical way of running the stations).

Yet, was it beyond comprehension that some area leaders made half-hearted gestures at stopping industries because of some subconscious thought that they didn't want to offend the union leaders in the steelworks and power stations, because they knew they would have to deal with them again in the bars and enclaves of the TUC and Labour Party conferences. There was certainly a great deal of reluctance on the part of some area leaders to place themselves fully behind Arthur Scargill's leadership. This was hardly a recipe for ensuring a march to victory.

March, April and May had been the main picketing period of the strike. And, although, picketing would carry on as a routine to prevent the movements of stockpiled coal, there were to be exceptions to this, as was the case with Orgreave coke ovens near Sheffield.

When the Orgreave coke depot was being picketed in June, it was sending coke to Ravensgraig steel works in Lancashire. Labour MP Dennis Skinner once told me over the phone that there had been agreement with the T&G at Orgreave that no more coke would leave the depot during the strike. The local union leaders needed more time, it seemed, to organise the stoppage. However, this wasn't to be, as the massive events involving police charging unarmed miners was to prove.

For three days the police had allowed the numbers of pickets at Orgreave to build up while they stealthily amassed lorries doubling up as horseboxes, private hire buses full of additional police to take the miners on streamed into the area. It is now well known that the BBC newsreel coverage of the events at Orgreave was reversed and showed a sequence of events where miners charged the police first rather than the other way around.

Who provoked who? Miners don't need convincing otherwise. The police acted as agent provocateurs at Orgreave.

In June 1984 many Maesteg Miners were at Orgreave and many were shocked by the police tactics. With my lodge chairman and two other committeemen we travelled in smart suits up the M1 to attempt to get near the action at Orgreave.

We were stopped by motorway police on a slip road outside Sheffield. Questioned by them for some time, we decided they must have our number, so to speak, and we decided we had no option to return home by via country roads rather than face arrest and make our contribution elsewhere.

It was better to have the freedom to organise in a time of great upheaval than to end up in a police cell under a dubious charge.

Port Talbot

5 Organising welfare and support in the Llynfi and Afan valleys

Miners who had been banned from going near a mine or a power station were ideal candidates to organise fundraising in some of the big cities. It was, however, to be a major source of conflict between the old Communist Party left and the new young militant Miners' Broad Left, with the latter proving to be best organisers and fundraisers.

Miners who would not even have had the confidence to be bingo callers in the years leading up to the strike were now delivering articulate accounts of the need for the stand against pit closures, arguing effectively the miners cause and of the need for money, food support and help for mining communities and families. Many miners' speakers would encounter patronising invitations only to speak about the poor hardship of miners families so that it was easier to give money to support the miners. The real appeal was the cause of the strike itself. The speaker had to wrestle with his conscience more often than not to put the political and economic reason for the strikes as opposed to just an appeal to help because we were by then so poor as not to be able to feed or look after our people.

While we had done some fundraising in London in the early part of the strike, the Llynfi Valley Joint Lodges sent two significant delegations to the cities: One to Birmingham and one to Plymouth.

This had been at the invitation of the Labour Party Young Socialists (LPYS) in those cities, supported by backers of the Militant newspaper. The trade union and Labour movement in those areas was exceptional in its support. The LPYS and Militant facilitated and brought introductions to the wider movement in the UK. During the strike, miners from the Llynfi and Afan valleys raised more than £300,000 for welfare support for miners and their families. There was exceptional organising and planning to ensure fair distribution of the food parcels valued at £3.95 (any higher and social security would have been deducted from payments to miners' wives for their children). To this day legal proceedings are being organised to obtain rulings for the return of deducted social security benefits from striking miners' wives and dependants

Ken Smith, a member of the LPYS national committee and a journalist for the Militant newspaper, was among the first to help organise the miners support group in Maesteg and chaired it for the next six months, until November 1984. Idwal Isaac, my father also played a role (how could I stop him, he had worked in the mines for 14 years and had been an AUEW Convenor in Cowley and in Silent Channel - a local car components company). He became its secretary, as well as being a local councillor. When Ken left to move to London in late 1984, Idwal was then elected as chairman of the miners' support group. Donna Jones from Abergwynfi then became its secretary and Shirley Wells a local school teacher and Labour Party member who supported the Militant retained the position of the group's treasurer.

Sustaining levels of fundraising for the two valleys

In the year of the strike the support group only once asked for money from the central NUM fund in Pontypridd, which itself had amassed a significant fund. They had raised more than £320,000. A sum of £20,000 was requested at the tail end of the strike because it was costing £7,000 a week to provide food and support to the miners and their families.

I am of the view that this was a remarkable demonstration of organising resilience, planning and forbearance in the face of the hostile forces organised by the state and also the obstacles placed before them by some in their own union.

Donna recalled in a recent book launch in Afan Argoed how it was all new to them. Idwal was too political, she recalls: "He said to me when we met Port Talbot Council... leave the talking to me.... after a while the council complained this is too political.... can anyone tell us what you need". Donna then explained their plight - "not enough money to pay their insurances and provide enough food for the children. Then the councillors said they understood and gave us £5,000." Peter Clements and Bobby Potts were to find the same kind of response when they were fundraising in the Midlands. It was easier to allow the pull on the heart strings of conscience than to listen to the case for retention of jobs and pits in the mining industry.

They became skilful at explaining the case as well as the need to alleviate the poverty of being on strike. Local councils could respond to the appeals about the problems of miners meeting their bills and having food in their bellies and a roof over their heads before doing anything about the miners cause itself.

Donna and Idwal were to create a bond of comradeship that would last the strike and beyond. What she said, she said fondly of her memories of her role as Llynfi Valley Miners' Support Group Secretary. When I asked Idwal about this he smiled and said: "We talked a lot over the phone and I arranged regular meetings... there was never any disagreement... we all had our jobs to do!"

Donna went on to say: "When Phil White (St John's NUM Compensation Secretary in charge of welfare in Llynfi and Afan Valleys during the strike) asked me for help because we didn't have enough volunteers at Christmas to organise the distribution of toys and gifts of clothing and household goods from Germany... my sister took over and organised it all." This is how solidarity works.

Miners' support groups expand throughout the valleys

The miners support groups expanded into all the valley communities. They were never called women's support groups in the Llynfi and Afan valleys as in other areas. In some areas the women's support groups tended to have an independent existence from the Lodges. In the Llynfi and Afan Valleys the Joint Lodges Strike Committee and the Miners' Support Group were inseparably linked.

While the support group had autonomy of operation and action, they did so within the parameters laid done by the strike committee. They organised soup kitchens where striking miners and pickets could get a daily breakfast or lunch.

As well as Nanty Library, where the food parcels were made up, there were other centres opened during the strike in Garth, Llynfi Lane Hall, Glyncorrwg, Cymmer and Gwynfi. Food parcels were distributed as well via these centres where single miners could get food and was a place to meet and chat and provide mutual support. These were manned by women and men from the miners' support groups in Garth, Maesteg, Nantyffyllon, Caerau, Abergwynfi, Glyncorrwg and Cymmer.

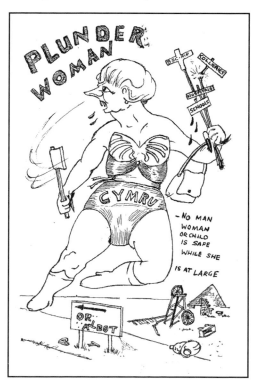

There are too many to name all of them but some key figures in the work of the support groups that were springing up in the local communities were Pam and Dave Walters in Glyncorrwg, assisted by Julian and Mary Hart. Pam and Dave were secretary and treasurers. Other miners' wives, whose husbands worked at Blaenant Colliery, were also involved.

In the Maesteg area there was Teresa Parry, Eirlys Furlong, Beryl James, Kath Morgan, Nesta Thomas, Lynda Sullivan, Linda Williams, Louise Pye, Vi John, Karin Clements, Jan Dare and Mitzi Sedgebeer (sadly no longer alive) among the dozens who were involved - my apologies to any who have been left out.

There were also those who weren't miners' wives but who gave their all during the strike, such as Shirley Wells and Helen Davies, Kath Williams and Ceri John (Reeves) from the Maesteg Labour Party Young Socialists and Gary Bevan and Hazel Gittings from Valley and Vale Arts.

The main organisers in Blaengwynfi were Donna Jones and her sister, and Anita and Colin Day. Colin was Craftsman's rep on the Lodge Committee.

Phil White recalls that he felt one of the most interesting things to come out of the Afan Valley support group was that the Co-op store in Blaengwnyfi where the group purchased its food from for the Afan food parcels closed during the strike. The store was then taken over as community coop store and run by Donna and others from the support group.

Phil said that "an initial empowering of the women via the miners support group gave them the confidence to run a community store, and I think that would have been unlikely to have happened if the strike had not taken place."

For many of those involved, the first few months of organising the support groups were a whirlwind. Ken Smith recalls some of his experience during the early days:

"I have many vivid memories of the strike, such as delivering food parcels at close to midnight on a Friday night, or staying in a striking miner's family's house towards the end of the strike on a bitterly cold night and the family had no coal or other source of fuel and all of us - men, women and children, and dog, huddled together on a sofa with a duvet thrown around all of us just to keep warm.

There were funny moments as well. There was the time when a single miner asked to swap flour and potatoes from his food parcels for more packets of processed peas. Some of us were a bit bemused by this and asked why to get the reply that it 'was to keep the pigeons alive, so, we weren't just a support network for the miners and their families but we were supporting their pigeons as well.

But there was a serious side to all of this - there had to be for the miners and their families to survive. One estimate I saw said that more than £60 million was raised for the miners and their families during the strike.

To do justice to all the activities of the support group would require a book in itself, but I think there are some points that can illustrate the work that was done, almost in a military fashion, by the supporters.

After a few months there were more than 10 support groups each having their own meetings and we used to convene a meeting with one rep from every local group on a Sunday, at 3pm, to ensure a democratic running of the groups and to reinforce the link to the Llynfi and Afan Valley NUM joint lodges which Ian was the secretary of.

At those meetings we would start with a general report from the NUM, usually from Ian or Phil, or one of the other lodge committee members. Then we would go on to discuss a general report on the activities of the support group, usually given by myself, and then have reports from each of the support group areas. Then we would discuss the finances, social activities, jumble sales, rotas and collections and so on, and everyone went away with a task - or half a dozen tasks in some cases. Often there were other things as well such as coaches to demos and miners' wives from Maesteg were the first to organise their own picket, outside the Margam entrance of Port Talbot steelworks.

The main support group centre in Nanty had an evening rota as well as people being there during the day - this was to ensure that, like the lodges, we were always contactable. During the early days the phone never stopped ringing. In my notebooks from those days I have one entry that shows on May 8, 1984, 350 food parcels were made and distributed. I am sure that at the height of the strike we were giving out more than 500 food parcels a week.

The fundraising work of the joint lodges and the support groups meant we could always fund our own way until the end of the strike. It was monumental effort too where fundraising was done by miners, their wives and their supporters outside local factories and workplaces. Everyone had official accreditation from the lodge and there were collections outside most workplaces on a Friday. There were also food trolleys outside local shops for donations, and I remember the manager of the Co-op in Caerau being particularly helpful.

All in all, this meant thousands of pounds were being handled every week. I have a note that one week Shirley and I had gone over the books and there was a discrepancy of 50p and we put that in ourselves to make sure there was no hint of maladministration.

"On May 9, 1984, my notes show that we paid out £628 - £539 in food, £85 for buses to go to demos, and £13 in petrol to Billy Pye and myself for the distribution of parcels to outlying areas.

"On May 23, my notes show that we paid out more than £1,000, most of which was for food but we did invest £1.35 to buy a collecting bucket.

"This is how it went on week after week, but it wasn't down to just a few individuals, it was a collective effort and an inspirational display of working-class solidarity that has never left me and never will."

This period was also a time of great public expression of support for the miners. Many organisations, local and national were to join in with St John's and other lodges to provide practical and material support for the action.

A meeting was called to set up a miners' support group early in the strike. In fact, it is claimed by those who took part that it was probably the first of its kind in the UK. Ken Smith, offered his considerable organisational skills in helping to organise meetings and prepare the way for the setting up of a miners' support group and other support networks throughout the trade union movement both locally and throughout the UK and abroad.

Wherever the ideas for miners' support groups and women's support groups came from, these ideas were put into practice early on in the dispute. We had anticipated the creation of this type of community support group for miners from our strike experiences in 1981 and 1983. I had read the accounts of the 'local action committees' of the 1926 general strike and miners' lock-out. I was keenly aware following the rejection of the idea of a national ballot that we were in for a long haul!

We had to raise the bar in terms of reaching out for support in the communities and in the wider movement.

That's why jealous types from the old British Communist Party and its Eurocommunist wing bleated like lost lambs to Emlyn Williams and George Rees that St John's miners were taking over Birmingham and Plymouth and had sent rank-and-file miners and lodge committeemen to set up support networks in the union and Labour movements in those areas during the strike. Phil White was later to recall that there were two camps struggling for control of the strike in South Wales and the UK – the new miners broad left and the old communist left. The miners broad left was the most active, imagination and innovative in its organising skills. There were of course those who straddled in between the two movements.

The Llynfi and Afan Valley miners were to gain a reputation for punching above their weight wherever they went. They were vocal and articulate – such skills had been encouraged by the young leadership in St John's and elsewhere in the valleys.

Birmingham the fundraising activities - two approaches put to the test.

Arfon Evans, who was the craftsman's rep on the South Wales Miners Executive, 'got the nod' from Kim Howells and Emlyn Williams to be the official South Wales NUM fundraisers in Birmingham. Evans had complained that Ian Isaac, a colleague on the South Miners Executive Council, was a "Militant supporter" and was carving up the country for his lodge and district.

I had to become immune to these jealousies, which were really a backroom gripe resulting from lack of imagination and foresight. Emlyn Williams knew what he was getting when I offered my services. He was one of the very few men who deserved the recognition of being a great South Wales Miners leader. Emlyn died a few years after the strike.

He didn't get to see these former 'Communist' complainers become religious converts, salesmen and contract managers. Other Communist members resigned and sought the political shelter of the Labour Party, particularly after the strike, and some became Labour MPs. All was forgiven for the former Communist Party NUM leaders. From what was once the most proscribed party in Britain, it and its former members who left in droves, had become the acceptable converts to the emerging New Labour "enterprise" of the 1990s.

While the official NUM team from the Maerdy Lodge sat in trade union offices waiting for money, cheques and letters of support to come in, St John's miners, led by Alan Williams a committeeman from St John's Lodge, went out into the factories and wider movement in Birmingham, and later onto the streets outside shopping centres and railway stations appealing for money and support. Alan was a formidable opponent and a trusted friend. He was supported by many rank and file miners from St John's including: Gwyn Harris, Alan 'legs' Stephenson, Peter 'two dogs' Clements, Bobby Potts, David Hookings, who also went to Plymouth with Lee Blackmore - all forthright personalities in their own right who were the salt of the miner's earth.

David Hookings was to become the official representative of the Llynfi and Afan Valley Joint Lodges in Plymouth, even though he was a rank-and-file member and not an official of the lodge itself. He was an example of those who stepped up to the plate and became official spokesmen of our lodge without portfolio.

They held principle in their minds and a willingness to work in their hands and hearts. Memories of my association with these men will remain with me for the rest of my life.

Eventually in Birmingham, despite attempts by the likes of Arfon Evans to create bad feeling between the two teams of South Wales miners, a sensible relationship and understanding was reached, between Terry Williams of Maerdy Lodge and St John's Lodge committeemen around Alan Williams, Peter Clements, Colin Scourfield, Alan (Legs) Stephenson, Bobby Potts and rank-and-file miners such as Gwyn Davies, 'Lux' and Richard "Zac" Williams!.

Further reading about Birmingham and the miners' strike can be obtained through the book by Paul Mackney, who at the time was secretary of Birmingham trades council and who later went on to become general secretary of the college lecturers' union Natfhe and UCU. Paul graphically described some of the activities of St John's miners in Birmingham. The reference in his book about me being "'a bastard" is I believe not in good taste, even though it was supposed to have been uttered by a Maerdy lodge official!

The fundraising teams from various parts of the South Wales coalfield met every Friday night to iron out any difficulties over a pint in a bar in central Birmingham. See how miners settled their differences when left to get on with it without interference from others' petty agendas. By sheer force of personality these men showed a tenacity of resolve, inventiveness and a newly discovered talent for public oratory and organisation that went on to achieve massive support - having had only the simplest of instructions to go to Birmingham and make contact with the TASS union, the Trade Union Research Unit (TURC) and built a network of support for the Llynfi Valley miners and their families.

I had been ordered by Emlyn Williams to withdraw them from Birmingham – but you know the old adage: "They wouldn't listen to me Emlyn, when I asked them to come home… they stayed up there despite my pleas"!

A St John's miner or a miner from the Llynfi or Afan Valleys could be seen somewhere in Birmingham and Plymouth from April 1984 to March 1985. They raised an average of £600 a week net of expenses (they were allowed £6 per day expenses – all above board and recorded during the strike. The money was spent on welfare and relief work in the community. The Llynfi and Afan Valley Miners support group raised £320,000 in the miners strike. £20,000 was requested from the South Wales area fund administered by Eric Davies, a colleague on the South Wales Miners Executive. Llynfi and Afan Valleys were self sustaining during the strike. It was a magnificent effort!

Every penny was spent of food parcels and soup kitchens right to the end.

It took some organising against very parochial thinking from some quarters. A scene erupted in Plymouth where the St John's Lodge had set up a presence, in what was effectively a Tory area in parliamentary terms. We had received an invitation to speak in Plymouth at the beginning of the strike and I was able to get a toehold in the local polytechnic through the NUS.

Again the personality and talents of men like Vic Sedgebeer, David Hookings, Kelvin Morris, Lee Blackmore, a miner called Lux, and again Bobby Potts, later in the year, organised a network of support from the union and Labour movement and the wider public that was to be sustained throughout the dispute. Vic Sedgebeer, the local COSA secretary was put in charge to involve him and his men directly in supporting the strike.

Again attempts by reactionary types within the NUM HQ in Pontypridd sent the Taff Merthyr Lodge to Plymouth to set up the official team from the NUM for the area. We had already set up a network of support in the Cohse and GMB unions as well as local working men's clubs. Merthyr Vale's attempts to organise fundraising in Plymouth came to nothing within a short period of time. The Llynfi and Afan Valley miners were there to stay for the duration.

Again, it was the superior organising skills and sheer will to achieve recognition and support that won through. It was costing the area large sums of money to send official representatives to the West Country when the Llynfi Valley paid the basic subsistence from the proceeds of the team's activities in Plymouth – all accounted for by Shirley Wells and Ron Roberts (vice-chairman of St John's NUM lodge), two of the most honest and dignified individuals I have ever had the pleasure to meet when it came to handling money. They raised and dealt with thousands of pounds for the miners' support group towards assistance for miners and their families.

I have in my papers a copy of a leaflet for a public meeting organised by Drake Ward Labour Party on Tuesday, June 19, 1984 at the Co-op rooms, Western College Road, Plymouth:

"Come and hear the miners from the Affan and Llynffi valleys (note the quaint misspellings). *Their one remaining coal mine is now listed for closure but unemployment in the Afan valley is already at 63 per cent. Only 26 remain in South Wales and Macgregor plans to close 20 of these."*

When the miners' support group was formed all officers of the support group were to be either miners' wives, relatives or activists from the broader movement in Maesteg and the Afan Valley and beyond.

Going global

Maesteg miners always thought global and acted local wherever they found themselves during the strike, home or abroad. Satellite support groups had been set up in Bridgend, Glyncorrwg and Abergwynfi in the Afan Valley. The Maesteg Joint Lodges adopted miners from other collieries who lived in the Llynfi and Afan Valleys. Vi John - later to be become a significant activist for the miners' continued struggle, and women's issues in Wales in the 1990s - was a product of the Maesteg, Garth soup kitchen.

During the strike the NUM and the miners' support group as stated already raised more than £320,000 all monies were used for providing over 500 weekly food parcels worth £3.95p each, which was governed by the DSS as the maximum allowed as a gift. Single miners were not entitled to a food parcel. They were looked after by the breakfast and soup kitchens. They also opened kitchens for miners' families to have free or subsidised meals from breakfast through to lunch and tea. These kitchens operated in more than six sites in the Afan Valley -with the main ones being in Maesteg, Bridgend and the Afan Valley.

Others were at the Old Age Centre in Garth, the Welfare Hall in Llynfi Lane (later to become an award-winning residential home for the elderly), and various centres in the Afan Valley (an area I had a soft spot for because I was born in Duffryn Rhondda) I was more than happy that the Afan Valley was so well organised by Phil White, Donna Jones, her sister and others who volunteered.

However, it was always the Joint Lodges Strike Committee which would have the final say in the event of any disputes or major areas of strike policy. To ensure that this arrangement was both empowering to the miners' support group and consistent with the aims of the strike itself, compensation secretary Phil White of St John's

Lodge, was appointed by the strike committee as the NUM's official representative on the miners' support group.

Phil was to go on to play a vital role in sustaining morale on a day-to-day basis particularly towards the end of the strike when hardship was beginning to have a material effect on morale.

Ron Roberts was given responsibility for all finance transactions on a daily basis including ensuring that pickets were paid. Pickets or men on duty were paid £4 expenses per day local and £6 per day when out of the area.

Later in the strike, Ron was to play a vital role in making sure that where hardship was identified that he had the authority to distribute hardship money to cases brought to his attention both from official lodge sources and from individuals. To this day Ron's integrity in this matter is beyond reproach. I didn't have to adjudicate on a single case or handle a single dispute over Ron's judgements.

Neither the strike committee nor the miners' support group heard appeals concerning hardship - they were all referred to Ron. That's how much esteem he was held with throughout the valleys.

The influence of the miners' support group

The women of the miners' support group seamlessly integrated themselves in the day-to-day workings of the provision of soup kitchens, food parcels, fundraising and the organising of events to raise money and provide essentials support for their husbands, brothers, uncles, grandfathers. There are hundreds of stories of solidarity performed at a local level during the strike. They say that the real history of a community isn't in the written accounts but in the stories, tales, traditions and mores of the community as they pass the stories on from generation to generation.

The story of the Llynfi and Afan Miners' Support Group is an account worthy of being recorded in itself. Perhaps, one day, someone will write its history. This is but one short overview of the work of the group.

It was never called a women's support group, this was another structure again set up by Cath Jones and others in Cardiff. Vi John from Garth, Maesteg, played a very active part in the work of the South Wales women's support group for many years after the strike. Vi has become a character recognised by hundreds in her local community and thousands throughout the Welsh and British coalfields. She is unmistakable with her hat of badges and her fundraising efforts for many causes during the 1990s.

The miners of the Llynfi and Afan valleys owe a debt of gratitude to people like Vi John, Donna Jones, Anita Day, Shirley Wells, Teresa Parry, Eirlys Furlong, Linda Williams, Linda Sullivan, Jan Dare, Karin Clements and all the others in the Llynfi and Afan Valley, all the valleys of the NUM Maesteg District including: Garw,

Ogmore, Bridgend, Pencoed and the support groups of the Cwm and Coedely areas that I had links with, who made the work of solidarity with miners and their families seem effortless and fun. At the same time they generated a level of political consciousness that far exceeded those who held prominent positions at parliamentary, Local government and trade union leaderships who had sat on their hands in leadership positions in the 'trade union and Labour movement' locally and across the country.

The Afan and Llynfi valleys were as one. This had not been achieved since the 1920s when they last stood shoulder to shoulder against a common foe - the state in its guise of police, social security or as armed bodies of men.

6 The role of the state as summer sun shines

The police and the army represent the state. This became profoundly clear to miners and their families during the strike. Many other accounts and testimonials describe the role of the police during the strike. For my part, I will only relate to my own experience. On one occasion I had accepted an invitation from Tony Ciano, the young militant secretary of Cynheidre Lodge (four senior lodge officials left the industry just before the strike and it was left to Tony and other young miners to do the hard yards to represent the men many of whom were twice their age).

Cynheidre had been the scene of intensive picketing mainly due to the fact the Winding Enginemen responsible for operating the cages in the shafts were scabs and had been encouraged by the Notts working miners' committee to take an injunction out against the NUM. On a few occasions during the strike we picketed Cynheidre, and I'm proud to say that my uncle, John Ambrose, a retired traffic police inspector and police trainer and then a full time preacher with the Welsh Baptist Church, provided us with breakfast on more than one occasion in his Pontyberem Manse, a few miles outside Cynheidre.

Judges attempt to confiscate South Wales NUM funds

The state was up to its old tricks when it attempted to grab the South Wales Miners' funds.

By the summer, certain men in South Wales (winding enginemen) were being supported by the Notts working miners committee to take legal action against the South Wales area.

Their attempt to sequestrate (freeze or confiscate by order of the courts) the South Wales NUM bank accounts was fought against vigorously and attempts by bailiffs to take property from the area office was fought back. A crowd of more than 10,000 had gathered outside the Sardis Road NUM office.

I had agreement from Emlyn Williams to address the crowd from the balcony, and to keep the assembled crowd of supporters engaged. Speakers from all political parties spoke to the crowd. As well as myself, there was Brian Ingham, industrial editor of the Militant newspaper, and others from the Labour Party Young Socialists (LPYS). All were to call on the TUC to organise a one-day general strike in support of the miners and in defiance of the sequestration of the funds.

I chaired proceedings for over an hour from the balcony of the NUM offices where a demonstration of thousands had gathered. The LPYS had been holding their summer camp in the Forest of Dean and hundreds of them had come down to Pontypridd to support the NUM. Speaking through the megaphone I declared: *"The eyes of the country and the trade union and Labour movement are on us today... We call on the Trades Union Congress to organise a one-day general strike in support of the miners and against the action of the Law Lords sequestrating the hard-earned funds of the South Wales Miners".*

As the day went on the call for solidarity and a general strike in support of miners was more and more being articulated by speaker after speaker. Andy Bevan the Militant-supporting Labour Party National Youth Officer spoke for the youth of the Labour movement when he said: *"The youth of the Labour movement and young miners have shown their mettle and maturity and have joined in this strike to defend the mining communities, the mining unions, and the pride of the trade union and Labour movement. When the time comes young workers throughout Britain will answer the call."*

Emlyn Williams finally addressed the crowd from the bottom steps of the headquarters. He defiantly roared: *"They will never enter these premises... If the TUC won't call for a strike in support of our action then I, on behalf of the South Wales Miners, the most courageous of men, call on the wider trade union and Labour movement to call a general strike to force this government to withdraw the pit closures, to invest in the coal industry and allow our young men with families to continue to earn a living in the way they know how."*

Anyone who ever knew Emlyn will hear him calling out these words in his distinctive gravel-like voice with so much passion. He was so passionate and determined, that at the time I feared for his health. He smoked as if part of his opera of life. He believed in family, community, society and mankind – it coursed through his veins. That is how I felt at the time.

Fun in the sun

It had been a long hot summer during the strike. The support group organised fetes and gala days to keep up morale. It felt good to be in the hot weather not doing the normal routines of work. However, for the activists and lodge leaders it was a hectic time. Many rank-and-file miners learnt the art of oratory having been asked to speak at meetings up and down the country and in many instances abroad as well.

We organised a sports gala day at Maesteg Rugby club in July 1984. Thousands marched around the town and up to the playing field and the bars of the Maesteg RFC. It is the only time in the history of Maesteg RFC when the pitch was used for a sporting occasion in support of a national strike. Without knowing it, the committee and officers of Maesteg RFC, had made history that day by granting permission on a free basis to use the field for a miners gala and sports day. Races were held. Rugby games were held and they were preceded by an appeal by me, Emlyn Williams, and our guest speaker Dennis Skinner MP, to stand firm and spread the word in support of the miners. Afterwards I took Dennis for a pint in the Sawyers Pub in Maesteg.

It was a wonderful summer's day and we were thirsty. He told me about Orgreave, that momentous event on June 18, 1984, and he said that the NUM virtually had an agreement from the T&G on site that this was to be last of the shipments of coking coal to Ravenscraig. I will never know who the controlling mind behind that event was. I don't think it was Arthur Scargill who was compelled to be there later in the day because his office was only a couple of miles down the road in Sheffield.

Later in the summer I went to Stuggart in Germany as guest of the metal workers union and to Stockholm in Sweden as a guest of the Swedish Young Socialists. I spoke in a number of trade union and political meetings. On both occasions I returned with hundreds of pounds and gifts for the miners support group.

The cranes at Port Talbot Steel works – a small story of a marooned Spanish coal vessel

July was the time of the cranes being occupied at the Margam Steelworks Harbour. Charlie had come from Pontypridd with another request for involvement in what I thought was another prank at the time. He said he wanted 12 men to volunteer to drive down to the steelworks (he and I had posed as NUR officials the week before to find out in the stevedores canteen when the next ship carrying coking coal was due in).

The NUM lodge men hired a mini bus and drove to the Number 3 gate just as the guard had changed hands at 9.58pm at the barrier. Some of the men tied the security guards hands with telephone cable having ripped it out of its jack plug. They then proceeded to the cranes.

We knew that the three cranes (which are still there to this day) would be on rails and drawn together. They were then ready to offload the ship when it docked.

They weren't the only miners who had hired mini buses that evening, as will become clear. The following morning I visited the site to be met by a Mr Ian MacGregor the Chief Constable of the British Transport Dock Police who shared his name with the chairman of the NCB. He inquired how many men were up the cranes. I said I would check with the president for him. I told him that the president didn't know how many because he had not organised it. It was a spontaneous act by the rank-and-file!

He said he thought there must be at least 30. I ventured no opinion at that point. He then turned to me and said: "You know after this is over I will tell you something that will surprise you"

I replied: "You know when this is over I will tell you something that will surprise you." I had a surprise for him too.

I made a number of visits over the next 68 hours to the ladders of the cranes to talk to the men. I had to accept responsibility for the situation even though I had not organised it. I was concerned for the welfare and safety of the men. I took cigarettes, a radio, and a few messages from loved ones and so on.

After 48 hours an injunction was placed on the South Wales NUM and delivered to the docks. I undertook to place the injunction on the ladder steps near where the men had put barbed wired preventing further access to the cranes. The ship, a Spanish-registered vessel, failed to offload its coal because it had to meet the tide for Ravenscraig Steelworks the following morning, so had no time to offload. This was a small victory for the miners involved but it came at a cost.

I negotiated with Ian Macgregor (who shared the same name as the NCB Chairman) that the men would come down from the cranes and be provided with a mini bus for each of their respective lodges, and that they would be allowed to go to their local police stations to be processed for trespass. Later charges of criminal damage were laid against them because a few scaffold poles were thrown towards the holds of the ships to keep them closed and police search lights that were trained on the cranes overnight.

It then came the time to reveal our respective surprises. I asked him what he wanted to tell me.

He said his wife had been the secretary for Will Paynter, general secretary of the NUM during the 1960s, and she had continued to work for the NUM at its Euston Road, London HQ until she had recently retired in her 50s.

Well, I said, my surprise was that you know you agreed to provide mini-buses? 'Yes', he said. Well, I said, we need 14 because there are 112 men up on those cranes. He was flabbergasted.

The men came down in the morning, 68 hours after climbing the cranes. They were somewhat forlorn. Each went to his lodge's marked up mini-bus. As far as I know they were all treated fairly at their destination as had been agreed. This Macgregor kept his end of the bargain. I can picture now how the men filed along the gantry now at sea level of the cranes as if they were prisoners of war about to be shipped away to a holding camp.

It became the largest number of defendants in a trial for the same offence in British legal history, so I'm told. Unfortunately, two men had previous convictions brought into account and were given custodial sentences. We visited their families to see what help we could give under the circumstances immediately following the trial. Any help required was provided.

Deputies stay in the colliery- refusing to go home!

During the autumn, when the NACODs deputies stayed in the pit because their safety to and from work wasn't guaranteed. This was a local misunderstanding. We had reinstated a picket line at the pit and the Nacods members would cross it and refused to be spoken to by the pickets. This resulted in a stand off between the men and the police at the crossroads near the colliery.

The police had special mobile units that were co-ordinated by the Chief of Police Association (COPA).

The police were kitted out in new shirts, they had the folded marks and creases still showing. These were either thugs or Army drafted in for the occasion. I had every intention of defusing the situation when I walked among our ranks along the forked roads to the pit appealing to the men not to be provoked.

William John, a pit overman, recalls how the police were stationed hiding behind the pit, having been positioned there in the early hours of the morning. "It was a question of dignity for us…. we didn't need to have an escort out of the pit as safety men because the NUM had sanctioned our work….I think they (the colliery manager, NCB and police)… thought things were too quiet at St John's and wanted to stir things up."

We won the day. No-one was hurt and after negotiation by Nacods we left the pit peacefully (with a few cheers from the boys who knew them all very well). They were of the same mining culture and families.

They had more in common with us than the imports of police drafted in and newly recruited police up for a 'ruck' with the St John's miners. I'm pleased to say that apart from a few skirmishes that Nacods and the NUM resolved to end the situation peacefully even though the colliery manager's car was turned over - an act I didn't condone. Trevor Bond said that after that he felt it was personal. I think all the efforts he put in to lure men back to work were personal!

7 Autumn sets in

NACODS, the deputies union, and the strike

On September 28, 1984, 17,000 pit deputies voted 82.5 per cent in favour of striking against the decision of the NCB to stop the pay of deputies who refused to cross picket lines and in opposition to pit closures and a breakdown in conciliation procedures between themselves and the NCB.

In St John's, all bar three or four of the deputies and overmen voted in favour - a mirror reflection of the national vote. Peter McNestry and Ken Sampey, general secretary and president of Nacods respectively, however then sat on their hands and prevented implementing the action because they, according to their own rule book, allowed the decision to become timed out.

They continued to negotiate their own version of an agreement against pit closures which was the final de facto agreement when the strike ended (because the NUM refused to sign the agreement). The Nacods ballot result was declared null and void when more than three weeks had elapsed, within which according to the union's rules a strike had to be implemented.

A further ballot would be necessary. But by then the embarrassment factor had kicked in and a further ballot would not be called. Either the general secretary and president were unaware and naive about the contents of their own rule book and rule on a time limit for legitimacy for strike action, or they deliberately played for time in the calculated hope that the appetite of deputies and overmen for strike action would wither away or a vain hope that the NCB may have conceded!

Frustration and tragedy as the strike wears on.

On November 30, David Hookings, who was in charge of fundraising in Plymouth, was confronted by a demonstration of taxi drivers and ambulance men outside the GMB union building. A brick had been thrown smashing the office window where David was sat having just got out of bed.

David phoned to ask what the hell was going on. A taxi driver, David Wilkie, had been killed by a concrete block being thrown from a bridge which hit the taxi resulting in his death. Two friends Dean Hancock and Russell Shankland had spent most of their time during the strike walking the mountains with their dogs but felt the need to respond to a call to increase the picketing effort for men returning to work in Trelewis Drift. David Williams, the passenger, continued to break the strike and go to work after the incident.

Tempers, frustrations and desperate actions were creeping in to the conduct of the South Wales miners, who had always prided themselves on have a measured approach - preferring communication, contact and intelligent dialogue with other workers and those going back to work rather than desperate tactics such as was displayed that day.

David Hookings was exceptionally brave in agreeing to speak with the taxi drivers and ambulance men from the steps of the GMB Union building. He began by expressing his sincere condolences to the families of the man who had been killed. He also unreservedly condemned the action of anyone who had been involved with or committed such a despicable act and if anyone had encouraged or authorised miners to perform this despicable act.

South Wales miners, in particular, were not afraid to stand up for themselves and fight if necessary but they were never bullies. If they ever witnessed bullying them would always intervene to prevent it spreading. While we understood the frustrations of certain sections of miners such acts were never to be condoned.

The TUC's lack of action

Norman Willis and the TUC general council had only given a couple of calls for "days of action" in support of the miners. These mainly involved extended lunchtime meetings or non-shift workers holding demonstrations in support of the miners.

The TUC ignored all calls for a one-day general strike. We continued to call on the TUC to organise a one-day general strike that would have galvanised the movement into solid display of solidarity with our causes. To say that the TUC sat on the fence for the whole of the strike is an understatement. These union careerists who had already achieved their lifetime appointments, their version of socialism, let the miners and their own members down. The railwaymen's pay dispute was settled quickly, the car workers' demands were met. Up and down the country disputes in most sectors were settled in favour of the unions. This reflected an orchestrated Government intervention in industry instructing the managers to settle any disputes that had the potential to run in parallel with the miners' strike.

Later in the strike there was a major rally held in the sports hall at the Afan Lido, Port Talbot, with more than 5,000 people in attendance. As well as Arthur Scargill and NUM general secretary Peter Heathfield, TUC general secretary Norman Willis was in attendance to show the TUC's "solidarity" with the miners. Within minutes of him starting his speech, above the audience an agile young miner had climbed the gantries in the massive hall and tied a hangman's noose over the rafters symbolising what should be done to the TUC. It got a huge cheer from the audience who laughed their approval. It was just a prank, but the media made a meal of it, trying to make out that the miners had become desperate by resorting to such symbolism. In the heat of battle these bizarre moments occur. It had no bearing on the strike but it did show how much the miners "had not appreciated" the support provided by Norman Willis, general secretary of the TUC at the time.

8 Standing firm

I n November I attended a special NUM conference in Sheffield. The following is an extract from the report of the Special Delegate Conference held on Monday, November 5, 1984, in the City Hall, Sheffield. This was the first time I had addressed a national NUM Delegate conference and I was nervous to say the least!

Mr. I. Isaac (South Wales): "I believe that this time, obviously, is a crucial period for our union, but I do think, listening to one or two faint hearts today, we should not forget the talents that have been released among our own members in the course of the last eight months. Many mineworkers have learned the art of organising, have learned the art of picking up the telephone, getting in contact with people and getting things done, and I believe that that is now what we need to do in order to take this strike forward.

They have learned the nuts and bolts of the organising of the strike, and I believe that we have got to release that now from this point on.

There is at the present time a small break in the ranks of the South Wales miners. Eighteen men, organised by the National Working Miners Committee, so-called, although one of them has recently been on the sick, Tony Ollman, but eighteen went in an organised fashion this morning to Cynheidre Colliery and in the furnacite plant also one went in. Our decision, as an Executive Council, is not to bow the head in this situation, but we have now called for the withdrawal of all safety men from the South Wales coalfield as and from this morning, including the Mines Rescue Station at Dinas and Loughor. (This was later rescinded for obvious reasons of safety)

We hope that we will hold the fort, because it will demonstrate that underlying these organised attempts by the Working Miners Committee the mood in South Wales particularly and in other areas is as has been said by other delegates, to be one of confidence in winning this dispute.

It has been mentioned before the 'general worker' is on our side. Right enough, it is not just going to be power stations, although in the issue of the power stations, I think we have to maintain the contact that we have had with the men in the power stations. We have got to have miners making new friends with power workers. If necessary, we have got to influence the TUC guidelines from below, and that means that we have got to adopt the same military-style campaign that Thatcher is now doing in places like Harrogate and Longmoor, where there are masses of lorries in order to take coal from the pitheads. We have to adopt the same strategy as them and mobilise our men as we did in the early months of this dispute in order to maintain these agreements, for example, there is an agreement in the West Country now where we have limited the CO_2 going into the power stations.

That type of thing has got to be maintained. Where we have got contact in the Midlands, we have got an agreement where coal is not going to go in or fresh coal is going in, then we have got to maintain those friendships in order to maintain those agreements. The Trent Valley power stations, I believe, are very strategically placed as far as the National Grid is concerned, because I understand that it does not necessarily feed Yorkshire and is not capable of feeding that area of the country if there was a boost in power needed.

"*But as well as the five rallies [the leadership had planned five major rallies to maintain support in the coalfields], I believe that we have also got to get out and convince our communities, as has already been said, but also that we have got to make sure that those in attendance at the five rallies are those men who have not, for one reason or another, been able to picket during the course of the dispute. When there are food parcels being distributed, I believe that the leaflets and the word of mouth should go out in order to make people come along to that particular rally.*

I would like to conclude by saying this, that as well as the power stations we have got to restate the economic argument about keeping our pits open as well as the political arguments. For example, the fact that in the 'Economic Aspects of the Coal Industry Dispute' pamphlet produced for this union by Andrew Glyn, it shows quite clearly that every single pit in this country is an economic socially viable unit, as far as this economy is concerned. I believe we have got to learn the language of that type of pamphlet, and again put that out to our members and also to the general public. Because we have come too far to throw it all away, and I am not, and indeed none of the South Wales miners, are going to hand over our industry to the likes of MacGregor and to the likes of all those private sharks who are waiting around the corner to defeat the miners' union. They will go in for the kill as far as the mining industry is concerned, and, yes, they will go in for the kill as far as the rest (of industry) *is concerned.*

"*So my appeal finally is, for us to keep our heads up, and I think that if we keep going we are bound to win. With 'General Winter' on our side we cannot lose.* (Applause).*"*

Upon reflection General Winter was certainly not enough. Those were my thoughts at the time – somewhat optimistic but never the less an attempt to raise morale for the continuation of our fight to defeat the NCB and the Government.

The 'mad' economics of pit closures

We clearly had to get our arguments across. Andrew Glyn - referred to in my speech at the conference - was clear in his exposition of the economics of the mining Industry. He was sought after by the NUM, the Labour Party and even the TUC. Such was the clarity of thinking of a Marxist economist like Andrew.[1] It would be remiss of me not to mention some of the economic aspects of the dispute.

Particularly because Andrew Glyn was a long-standing colleague and comrade, who I knew would be prepared to get involved and use the disciplines of economic analysis to assist the miners and their leaders in arguing their corner with the NCB and the Government.

Andrew stated that his pamphlet demonstrated, contrary to the Government's allegations, that the coal industry was "insolvent" before the dispute, that the production of coal in 1983/84 more than covered its production costs! It was indeed solvent!

He went on further to state that "closure of the so-called "uneconomic pits", far from benefiting the rest of society, would lead to higher taxation and lower living standards as a result of the loss of production involved. It is also argued that the same factor (mass unemployment) which makes closure of "uneconomic pits" extremely costly to the rest of society as well as the workers concerned, also makes investment in redeveloping existing pits *extremely* beneficial."

He concluded by stating that the best available estimates for the economic impact of the current (October 1, 1984) dispute shows that it is costing the equivalent of £5 per week for each person at work in the economy and has cost £3.5 billion so far. The average wage then was only £90 per week.

Andrew sent me a personally signed photocopy on October 24, 1984, inscribing it *"To Ian, best comradely greetings, Andrew 24.10.84"* (This is reproduced in the appendices).

New year - new challenges

Christmas was a sad time but we raised our spirits. We received a lorry load of toys and clothes from Germany. The women from both valleys came together and organised the biggest bazaar of clothes and toys that I have ever seen on the dance floor/hall of Nantyffyllon Institute. With its sprung floor, the venue is still available to this day.

We had a Christmas dinner and dance at the institute where we invited officials from all the areas who had helped us – Andy Richards from Fords, Nick Catterall from the GMB, and Trevor Parsons from the Cohse union in Plymouth. Trade unionists from abroad and from Birmingham all attended a celebration of the season and for us to show our appreciation for their support.

On January 23, 1985, eight miners went back to work in St John's defying the picket lines. We were aware that the colliery manager had been having secret meetings in the Oystercatcher Bar in Laleston, near Bridgend. We knew this because we had sent a couple of men to be a fly on the wall, at the event. The manager bought them all drinks and had a general chat with promises of protection and support and promises of early pays to affect the deal.

He had been phoning miners who lived in the outlying areas, away from Maesteg, Llangynwyd and the rest of the valleys. Porthcawl, Bridgend and Bryncethin were targeted.

One of those targeted, Roy Calender, had been a close friend and a work colleague of mine. We had done our coalface training together and his father was a high-ranking official with the CPSA union in London. His father approached me numerous times at union conferences to inquire how Roy was because we worked together.

Roy had been driving taxis for Village Cars, a local firm in Aberkenfig, during the strike. We took the view that if any miner could find a way of earning a living in many traditional ways as we knew them, then it was better that they be occupied and providing for themselves and their families, rather than breaking the strike or being subject to NCB, Government and media propaganda, which was being whipped up into a frenzy of mis-statements concerning numbers going back to work from January 1985 onwards in the South Wales coalfield.

Myself, Ron Roberts, Phil White and Vic Sedgebeer were sacked as a result of a meeting with Village Cars and Roy Calender. We were cited for intimidating a miner going back to work. Nothing could be further from the truth.

We visited Village Cars in Aberkenfig, and held a meeting with the proprietor. We assured him that we did not want to seek to prevent the miner concerned from driving his cars but would seek to boycott his company if he used his taxis to drive strike-breaking miners back to work.

We shook hands all round and that miner promised to return to the strike. But this was a promise he was later to break, alleging intimidation. We had tape recorded all the proceedings, as we did when the colliery manager invited us to a meeting at the pit, when he sacked us. The transcripts would have made interesting reading in a court of law, were we of a mind to claim damages had we remained sacked after the dispute.

Things start getting tough

In early February 1985, towards the end of the strike, the miners' support group insisted I had a food parcel for myself, my wife and three children. Having collected the parcel, I had a knock on the door later that evening from a striking miner who asked if he could borrow some money and have a bit more support.

I asked him in and talked about his circumstances and gave him our food parcel and some money. I had trained with him in work and had driven him to work over the years, he was a friend and comrade. What else could I have done? I also referred him to Ron Roberts, who I know helped him a bit more. It was getting tougher by the day.

The endgame

The executive council of the South Wales Miners had met the day before at a conference of lodge committees. The decision to recommend a return to work without agreement was a difficult one to make but for the reasons outlined below it was a decision I shared and participated in.

Below are extracts of a speech I made to the last conference of all lodge committees in Wales during the strike. It was a full conference of the South Wales NUM in Porthcawl.

I was called by the president to speak from the rostrum addressing 250 delegates from the lodges, I began by referring to those who wanted to fight to the last man.

There was no-one more willing to sacrifice than myself and that went for the majority of my lodge committee but the time had come to beat an orderly retreat.

"There are those who claim they are mandated to fight on and voted against a return to work. They were going to… "fight to last man", this was a reference to the depth of feeling among the Tower, Maerdy and Trelewis drift delegations.

I explained from the rostrum, why I was calling for an orderly return to work "without agreement".

"The prospect of the trade union and labour movement mobilising in support of the miners, in parallel action, had disappeared. Thatcher has settled with the car workers, railway workers, local authority workers and ensured that each section of the Labour and trade union movement was bought off either for their annual pay awards or settling their grievances and disputes on favourable term in each respective industry. The prospects of parallel action were now remote", I said.

Kim Howells approached me outside the Pavilion in Porthcawl where the conference had been held and said: "Well done that was a good speech and they listened". My reasons for the appeal to return to work without an agreement, however, had been based on entirely different reasoning than his.

My reasons for calling for an end to the strike were not based on giving up the fight. My reasons were based on the need to maintain the leadership of the lodges and the executive at a time when the miners had been abandoned by the TUC and the Labour Party, without prospect of any further material support. The prospect of victory had been taken away by the lack of such support and the fact that the press had by then (January 1985 in some accounts) reported that more than 50% of miners were now back at work defying their own union. We needed to keep the South Wales NUM intact to fight again another day. I lived daily among very brave and committed miners and their families and extended families. They would do anything asked of them even continue to make sacrifices to save the pit until the numbers actually on strike would have been the few and not the many . They knew by then that the miners' strike would not be won when Thatcher and the state had dug in, remained deaf to all appeals for settlement and witnessed the lack of support from the TUC and Labour Party every day in Parliament and elsewhere. The Tories mocked such weak leadership from Neil Kinnock and Norman Willis.

Either way this was the beginning of the last phase of the closure and destruction of the South Wales Coalfield. I took no sense of achievement from that speech – it was something I had to do in all conscience, I could not accept the responsibility for continued hardship in the mining community that I represented. They had been out on strike for a whole year. There are times even when the final defeat or victory is someway off that an army has to beat an orderly retreat. This was such a day.

General Carl Von Clauswitz once said: "You cannot be a general without an army"… "The best strategy is always to be very strong; first in general, and then at the decisive point. . . . There is no higher and simpler law of strategy than that of keeping one's forces concentrated… superiority of numbers is the most common element in victory. . . . Superiority . . . can obviously reach the point where it is overwhelming. . . It follows that as many troops as possible should be brought into the engagement at the decisive point".

I appealed to the conference: *"While the overwhelming majority of South Wales miners continued to remain loyal to their union and the strike, this was not the case in every other coalfield. The majority of English and Scottish Miners were now ignoring the picket lines with serious consequences for the cohesion of their communities and the NUM Nationally. We are in danger of losing the right to lead if something wasn't done to bring the dispute to an end.*

"The leaders of the trade union movement had willingly tied their hands behind their backs. We appealed to the conference to support the executive council recommendation. We came out with dignity together we go back with dignity together- intact as a union and as a fighting force". I stepped down from the rostrum and returned to the table where my lodge delegation of 14 men was sat.

The vote was carried to return to work. The national conference met the following day and recommended a return to work the following Tuesday.

We went back after two days of unnecessary delay, which allowed disgruntled miners a chance to make an independent stand on the basis that we are going back to work – "anyway what does a day or two matter" was some of their reasoning. It was my reasoning too: 'Why not stay out for two more days to establish the principle of all going back as one'.

I was baffled why this was the case? I understood why we would all go back together area by area. But to allow two days (Friday and Monday) as further days for new strikebreakers to return to work, to rub our noses in it, baffled me. I haven't understood that logic to this day. It meant that an additional 23 men out of 780 NUM members in St John's went back to work on the Friday and Monday.

I knew they were under family, personal and financial pressures but where was the dignity in defying your union for one or two days?

Perhaps it was a way of getting their own back, in a personal way, at some of the lodge leaders. For me the struggle was always bigger than any one man or any strike breaker, whether he broke the strike for one day or two months.

We went back to work under the banner of The Llynfi Valley Joint Lodges. St John's nor Coegnant had their own separate banners. Whatever we did publicly, we did together. I think that Caerau had its own banner at sometime, though I can't recall seeing it.

Back to work with pride and dignity

At 6am on a sharp, frosty, early March morning we marched the last half a mile to the pit. Buses and cars were left behind at the crossroads to the pit lane. Three hundred men marched back to work. It was uncanny but they knew their shift patterns, even though they had been out for a year.

We still had a fight on our hands. I asked to see the colliery manager and formerly declared the strike over for St John's and further said: "I still represent the men of St John's NUM, even though I am officially sacked, shall we accept the current situation?" He acknowledged what I had said. Two weeks later Terry Whelan, Paul Davies, myself, Phil White, Vic Sedgebeer and Ron Roberts returned to work.

An amnesty for sacked miners was reached in Wales, in contrast to the rest of the country. Emlyn Williams and Phil Weekes had come to an agreement. That was the measure of both men who had witnessed tumultuous events that tested their principles of fair play and justice to the limit. The fight to Keep Mining in Maesteg was about to begin.

1 The Economic aspects of the coal Industry dispute', prepared for the NUM by Andrew Glyn, Fellow and Tutor in Economics, corpus Christi College, Oxford and associate member Oxford University Institute of Economics and Statistics.

Part three:
The fight to keep mining in Maesteg

9 The battle to keep St John's open

Spring 1985 and back to work

THE PIT opened for work again on Tuesday, March 10, 1985. Me, Ron, Phil and Vic were reporting each day to the lodge office. After a couple of weeks it was announced that Emlyn Williams and Phil Weekes had agreed an amnesty for sacked miners. All bar the most serious offences were disregarded as being a consequence of the strike itself and men allowed to return to work.

The lodge committee continued to meet every two weeks and it was noticeable by now that it had changed again during the course of the dispute.

As well as lodge committee men such as Norman Dawkins and Jimmy Jones, who opted to finish on the redundancy offered by the board, other men opted to leave the lodge.

In keeping with the principle of not opposing faces closing where proven exhaustion of reserves was the case, the lodge agreed to a slimming down of labour at the pit to 450 men.

There were still no compulsory redundancies within the coal industry officially, but there was by now significant inducements for men to finish with much higher than the previous redundancy payments schemes. It was a myth that St John's NUM had decided against any redundancies at that time. It was a matter for each individual miner to decide whether to apply for redundancy or not. We appealed for sufficient numbers of men to remain at the pit to make it viable now that the South Pit would no longer be producing coal.

We had a pit to try to keep open on a slimmed-down basis. It was the resolve of the vast majority of miners to continue to refuse redundancies. The committee still held to the principle of a fighting union to keep campaigning to keep the pit open.

New lodge committee men took the place of those who had left the industry in the July of 1985. Men such as Peter "two dogs" Clements, Robert James, (his brother 'Floyd' also always supportive of the stand taken by the lodge) Robert Bevan and Alan "Legs" Stephenson helped to strengthen the lodge's resolve.

Later these men transferred to Bettws new mine. Bobby Potts a St John's lodge committeeman with a strong desire for trade union and socialist principles also transferred to Bettws new mine. Peter Clements became Bettws compensation secretary and 'Legs' Alan Stephenson took up a position on their lodge committee. In the 1990s he was to become shop steward and convenor in the Panasonic Factory at Baglan Moors in Port Talbot until it closed in 2007. Peter Clements spoke of his experiences in the strike at a meeting organised by the Socialist Party in Cardiff to commemorate the events of 1984-85, supported by Bobby Potts who had just recovered from a heart attack - 25 years on from the start of the strike and the experiences are still a lesson to a young audience of trade union and socialist thinkers. The guest speaker that night was Ken Smith recalling the support and stand taken by the Labour Party Young Socialists and Militant during the strike and subsequent struggles within the trade union and Labour movement.

Slimming down

The lodge took the view that all men over the age of 50 could leave the industry under redundancy or another scheme of benefit to them. We would slim down to 450 men from the 960 that there had been before the strike. We had 780 NUM members at the start of the strike, all the others belong to Nacods (The deputies union) and BACM (the managers union).

By October 29, 1985, 117 men had accepted redundancy (mainly over the age of 50), 140 had opted for transfers in the event that the pit would be closed.

Bettws Colliery took 49, Blaenant 39, Abernant 30, Lady Windsor 13, Cwm six and Maesteg Washeries three. There were, at that point, 324 NUM members left on the books ready to continue to fight and run the pit on a slimmed-down basis as proposed by St John's NUM Lodge.

All the work of the lodge was taken up ensuring the smooth transition during this period of slimming down. Sitting in with all men who were being consulted about finishing through redundancy, we never ducked any responsibilities to represent the men even as they considered leaving the industry. Lodge committeemen acted as witnesses in interviews for men who were being processed by the NCB industrial relations department. By July 1985, all those over 50 wanting to leave had left. This included any under 50 who opted to take redundancy.

It proved difficult getting down to the 450 figure because there was a general reluctance - despite the propaganda and inducements of money, lump sums and transfer payments of £800 - to go to another pit. As of October 29, 1985, there were 324 NUM men left on the books and circa 480 men in total left to run the mine, while 117 had accepted redundancy (mainly over the age of 50). There was sufficient manpower to run the pit through the Modified Colliery Review Procedure. We kept up the struggle to the bitter end.

Further issues on redundancy

I wrote to Terry Thomas, the miners' agent, concerning W H James, a test case for 20 other men. These men were due to finish on July 3 and were processed by the industrial relations department. A second batch finished on August 3, and were given six weeks' cash-in-lieu of notice.

The men felt strongly that it wasn't their fault that the NCB used the periods of notice as a device to encourage further redundancies in St John's Colliery - only 120 men out of 670 volunteered for redundancy, all the rest opted for transfers which proved to be a major headache for the NCB.

I requested that the miners' agent take this matter up with the manpower department of the NCB Llanishen HQ.

St John's NUM Lodge had to deal with the colliery review procedure yet again. The NCB wasted little time in hauling us before the gathering of the board's South Wales mining engineering elite. As mentioned before, these men were no doubt driven by their own vested interests in terms of pension lump sums and payments for running the industry down.

A pit visit by the executioner

Cliff (C J) Davies was such an individual, whose passion for closing pits increased after the strike. We escorted him underground to the B1 face and I addressed a tailgate heading meeting with the men of the coalface from the top of a Doscoe machine. Mr Davies didn't like that sort of impromptu expression of views and feeling from ordinary miners. It didn't fit with his sense of self importance, in that only people like him knew the mining engineering problems and the economic difficulties of keeping a pit like St John's open.

In the fight to keep the pit open. We organised a campaign called Keep Mining in Maesteg organised by the St John's NUM and Communities Action Campaign. Idwal Isaac became its Chairman. This group was the public link for the lodge to maintain its links with the large numbers of people who had supported us during the strike.

On May Day 1985, a traditional international workers' day and public holiday in many parts of the world, a rally was held in Maesteg. An astonishing mixture of leaders was brought together to address a meeting in the town hall. The large poster advertising the event, printed by Gibbs Brothers, announced:

St John's NUM and Communities Action Campaign Committee

Calls upon all Sections of the Llynfi and Afan Valleys to attend and Support

A MAY DAY PUBLIC MEETING

At the TOWN HALL, MAESTEG, MONDAY, 6TH MAY, 1985 at 11am

TO HEAR the CASE to KEEP St JOHN'S COLLIERY OPEN –

The LAST PIT IN BOTH VALLEYS.

Speakers:

GEORGE REES ,General-Secretary, NUM South Wales Area

RAY POWELL MP, Ogmore

JOHN MORRIS MP, Aberavon

DAVE NELLIST MP ,Coventry

IAN ISAAC, St John's Lodge Sec and EC Member

Support your local NUM and Labour Party in

KEEPING ST JOHN'S COLLIERY OPEN AND TO KEEP MINING IN MAESTEG

We call on all sections of the Community to

ATTEND THIS IMPORTANT MEETING – KEEP JOBS IN MAESTEG!

The town hall was full, with more than 600 people in attendance. I had pulled together left-wing, right-wing and middle of the road MPs, and particularly held those who were local MPs to account – for this occasion at least.

The campaign to ensure the meeting was a success was hard graft. How do you draw together people who had given their all for the previous year and ask for more effort, more campaigning, leaving no stone unturned in their efforts?

It was not for the want of trying. We were proving ourselves to be as expert as the managers who sought to buy into the run down of the British mining Industry.

I recall NUM national general secretary, Peter Heathfield, making a poignant remark at the NUM national special delegate conference the previous November in Sheffield, where I had spoken as a South Wales Delegate. (See part 2) Paraphrased he said: *"If the Government had announced the closure of individual steel works as part of the*

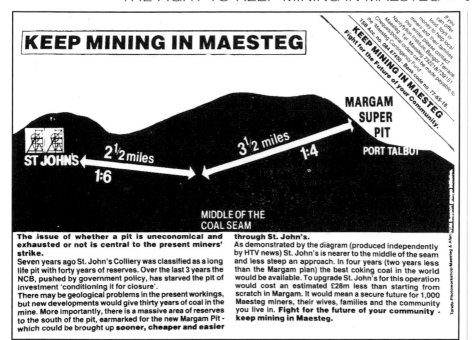

KEEP MINING IN MAESTEG

ST JOHN'S 2½ miles 1:6

3½ miles 1:4

MARGAM SUPER PIT PORT TALBOT

MIDDLE OF THE COAL SEAM

The issue of whether a pit is uneconomical and exhausted or not is central to the present miners' strike.

Seven years ago St. John's Colliery was classified as a long life pit with forty years of reserves. Over the last 3 years the NCB, pushed by government policy, has starved the pit of investment 'conditioning it for closure'.

There may be geological problems in the present workings, but new developments would give thirty years of coal in the mine. More importantly, there is a massive area of reserves to the south of the pit, earmarked for the new Margam Pit - which could be brought up **sooner, cheaper and easier**

through St. John's.

As demonstrated by the diagram (produced independently by HTV news) St. John's is nearer to the middle of the seam and less steep an approach. In four years (two years less than the Margam plan) the best coking coal in the world would be available. To upgrade St. John's for this operation would cost an estimated £28m less than starting from scratch in Margam. It would mean a secure future for 1,000 Maesteg miners, their wives, families and the community you live in. **Fight for the future of your community - keep mining in Maesteg.**

planned rundown in the steel industry would not Bill Sirs [general secretary of the ISTC union] call for your support. If the teachers were faced with the closing of schools in all parts of the country as part of a rundown in education provision, if they started closing hospitals without alternative centres for treatment or doctor's surgeries in places where people needed them wouldn't doctors call out for public support. The miners were not any different when faced with the cynical destruction of their industry."

We had proven the case against closures. The point was to have the support from all sections of the community to put a stop to it. We tried!

Linking up with local industries

The Campaign to Keep Mining in Maesteg:

Letter from British Tissues a Large Paper works near Maesteg.

We had written them a letter inquiring if the company had considered fluidised bed combustion systems for their production and heating requirements.

The reply: "Reference to your letter dated October 19 on the above subject. This will be given our attention and we will reply as soon as possible." EF Marker, Mill Manager [Within a year the paper mills had introduced a fluidised bed combustion unit. The coal came from elsewhere and not from local sources.]

I wrote numerous letters to trade unions and the Labour movement. It came as some surprise when one of my letters was answered by then Labour leader Neil Kinnock. Neil Kinnock had gained a reputation for sitting on the fence during the strike. He had made more than the occasional reference to the lack of a national ballot and many had felt that he had not done much for the miners during the strike.

St John's NUM press release:
"Mr Neil Kinnock, leader of the Labour opposition, who has studied the details of the NUM case to Keep Mining in Maesteg and oppose the closure of St John's Colliery has decided to visit the colliery at the invitation of its secretary Mr Ian Isaac."
The visit will take place on Friday, June 7, from 7.30am to 12.30pm.

Kinnock visits St John's and joins the campaign

Neil Kinnock kept to his word, and came to St John's Colliery on June 7, 1985. I confirmed that arrangements had been made with the colliery manager and with C J Davies, the deputy director of the South Wales Area of the NCB, that his visit would commence at 7.30 am with a welcome cup of tea and introductions, then to the baths to be kitted out in clothing suitable for walking underground.

We entered the North Pit at around 8.30am - an unusual procession of men with their overalls and pit helmets walked among the dusty coal drizzle as it blew in our faces from the upcast airflow of the North Pit.

Mr Trevor Bond (it was tradition to refer to colliery managers as Mr) Mr Cliff Davies, Neil Kinnock, John Reid, (Neil Kinnock's private parliamentary secretary), Charlie White and myself walked the mile and a half to the face to meet the men.

I made a point of ensuring that, as well as the opportunities to describe the situation in the mine by the managers and ourselves, that I would introduce Neil to every miner that we came across that day. Miner, Barry Merritt was one of those who made their feelings known when he referred to the sitting on the fence view that many miners had regarding Neil's position during the strike, as we walked past an electrical transformer station underground on the way to the B District. However, on this occasion I believe that Neil Kinnock was actually taking the opportunity to align himself with the struggle to keep pits open, and to ensure that if there was a case to remain open then he was supporting that case.

We came up around noon having talked to most of the men on shift underground that day. The manager and deputy director stayed in the background as we facilitated conversations with rank-and-file miners. Having later shared a cigarette with some of the surface workers, we held a press conference in the canteen where we put the case for keeping the colliery open. After some hospitality in the manager's

Kinnock at St John's

office we thanked them for their courtesy and for helping to ensure a comprehensive visit of the mine.

Neil Kinnock said in the South Wales Echo that evening: "The lodge is arguing for a reduced workforce and it seems likely that around 450 men will remain at the pit demanding to work the mineable reserves for a minimum of seven years in the North Pit reserves."

During his visit, Neil Kinnock suggested we hold an independent public inquiry. It was as if another light was switched on to illuminate the case against St John's closing. I had never heard of an independent public inquiry before.

That didn't matter, I embraced the idea with enthusiasm and resolve. Alan Fisher who was general secretary of the National Union of Public Employees (NUPE) who the previous year had been chairman of the Trades Union Congress (TUC) agreed to chair the inquiry.

Stephen Fothergill from Cambridge University and the Coalfields Campaign also agreed to be on the panel as did the Reverend John Morgans and Gareth Rees from UWIST [University of Wales Institute of Science and Technology.]

The campaign for an independent inquiry

We raised the money to set up the inquiry and ensure that all expenses were met - although none of the panel claimed any expenses.

I had contacted Phillip Squires, leader of Mid Glamorgan County Council, a man who had a reputation as being a powerful broker. He offered me the complete services of the council to host the inquiry.

I asked if we could hold it in the Mid Glamorgan County Council offices and he agreed without hesitation. His county clerk at the time was one of the most helpful individuals I have met. Today they are called chief executives. They have come a long way from the council clerk position.

We were offered the sound and

Ian addressing the Inquiry

a videoing facility of the council, and the inquiry was recorded by a stenographer. The final report, was the result of a painstaking gathering of material. Andrew Glyn gave oral and written evidence. I appeared before the inquiry to answer questions, as did Idwal Isaac, my father, who was the secretary of the campaign to Keep Mining in Maesteg. Bert Ramelson regional organiser in Wales and the West Country from the Communist Party also submitted written evidence as did many others.

Idwal won't thank me for saying this but he stuck it through to the end. Never once did he challenge any of the strategies or tactics of me or the lodge. He put it simply in a recent conversation I had with him: "I was there to do a job... to support the miners and their families... you and the lodge made the decisions I helped organised the support."

A few weeks later, when our campaign material was more refined, we were invited to the House of Commons to meet Neil Kinnock again, who having suggested that we might try to hold an independent public inquiry was now holding a reception to launch the inquiry's findings.

Ray Powell, the local Labour MP, also attended and we did the usual parliamentary things and took photos and got the press involved. We had the report printed by Gibbs Printers, our local family run printing company in Maesteg. David Gibbs was ever the editor, and he liked to get things like the grammar, spelling and syntax right. I had over the years spent many hours going over leaflets, posters and pamphlets with David, such as the one, Keep Mining in Maesteg, we circulated widely throughout Maesteg and Afan Valley as well as more widely around the country.

The inquiry's findings were circulated widely, with copies going to members of the House of Lords and House of Commons.

Notable replies included ones from Derek Ezra and Barbara Castle.

We were inching our way toward having our case heard. The new modified colliery review procedure allowed for the impact on communities to be taken into account. The following extract from the executive council of the South Wales NUM general secretary's report shows how progress was being made:

Modified colliery review procedure

"The National Secretary reported that they had been informed by Mr J Cowan on Monday evening, September 9, that the union's appeal on Bates, Horden and St. John's would now be held under Modified Review procedure provided that there has been agreement between the board and the unions prior to October 4, 1985. From the information given, it would appear that the Horden appeal will be held by Justice Medd and the St John's Appeal will be held by Steven Sedley QC, who are both chairman of the National Reference Tribunals.*

This information was noted.

George Rees commented: *"A further article appeared in the Financial Times concerning three Pits Horden, Bates and St John's. The mining unions had refused to meet with the NCB over the new Modified Colliery Review Procedure (because they feared it to be the start of a rapid pit closure programme. There was also disagreement of the composition of an independent panel to be chair by Lord Justice Medd and Mr. Stephen Sedley QC. The NCB insisted on six arbitrators – chosen from the Senate of the Inns of Court. The effect of all this wrangling meant that St John's didn't have its day in court."*

We did all we could to publicise the case for St John's. It kept our profile high in the public arena. We were by now in the New Modified Colliery Review Procedure. It would be revealed later that we had even been listed for review by a QC - Mr Stephen Sedley.

But the case never had a chance to be examined before the campaign by the NCB was intensified and dear old Cliff ('C J close um') Davies would be up to his old tricks, sending memos to the colliery manager to bring it to the men's attention that in view of the year lost in national insurance contributions during the strike that men could well lose benefit if they leave the decision to take redundancy or transfer to another mine if they leave it until after Christmas and New Year 1986. I felt it my duty to post an analysis of the complexities of the benefit system so that each miner would know where he stood. They would have been okay in every case according to my reckoning and I would have supported them. The propaganda of the NCB at the eleven hour was later to hold the day.

Day to day lodge business goes on.

"Dear Ian, have you any badges? – I'll pay for them".

A new phenomenon occurred during and after the miners' strike, that of badge collecting. I dealt with numerous requests for badges. The lodge had commissioned St John's NUM 1984-85 Strike Badges from a company in Birmingham.

After the strike, badges became a valuable collectors' item:

D J Brown Tyne and Wear

As a loyal member of Durham NUM Wearmouth Lodge No 1688, I'm making a commemorative plaque consisting of all strike and individual colliery badges. If you could supply me with any I would be very grateful. I will also be obliged to forward any monies needed. Thank you for your time.

Yours faithfully

D J Brown

N.B. Ticked off, no monies required.

G Young, Yorkshire

Wrote to Vale of Neath Lodge and they kindly sent me a badge and list of Lodge addresses. If your lodge has a badge would you mind helping?

W Glover

Acocks Green, Birmingham, April 25, 1985

From Gwyn Harris

Hope you're well. I'm writing to say that we raffled the miners' lamp you sent us. Let me know who to make the cheque out to for your campaign to keep the pit open. If you could somehow get me another lamp we can sell it for £20. I've had a number of requests for badges if you could let me have some we could raise some more money. Hope to hear from you soon.

Badge requests from: J S Pye, Rushden, N Hants; W Jex Mountain Ash; Dick Hall Ex Ruskin Col; Mansfield. Mr C Carter, Roberstown, Aberdare

Dave Hopper, Secretary, Monkwearmouth
Send us some badges and we'll send some of ours".
Yours fraternally, Dave
Agreed

Doug Broadfoot, Mansfield
I am a Notts Miner at Clipstone colliery who backed the 1984-85 strike . . . unable to get one of your colliery badges.
Agreed

Badges request: Roberts Shipstone, Notttingham; Paul Martin Brighton, E Sussex; Iain Chalmers, Cowdenbeath, Fife; John Hampson, Selby, North Yorkshire; L Stemp. Blyth, Northumberland; Chris Skidmore, Barnsley, South Yorkshire; P Martin, Brighton, E Sussex; W Shaw, Barnsley, S. Yorks.

Every request had a letter describing why the person wanted a badge and what their experience of the strike was.

There were many more requests for badges and I responded to every single one and sent a badge at no cost to the person requesting them. It was an honour to be asked. Other inquiries would include:

William Ronald Pascoe, Tondu, Bridgend
I send my union contribution for 1984 also my contribution card with SAE. I was 65 on 26-6-84 Do I still have to pay contributions or can I have honorary membership?
Sent Honorary Membership Card.

Mark Williams, April 1, 1985, Pontypool
I am a student studying business studies . . . I need to draw up an organisation chart of the NUM regionally and nationally. Please could you send me copy of such a chart or any information that you have to help me draw up a chart?
Send him Diary and Info on 'Keeping Mining in Maesteg'.

Meanwhile the day to day tasks of running the Lodge Office are dealt with:

Example Letter:
Mr. I Griffiths, Head of Housing, NCB Cardiff Rd, Nantgarw, Treforest.
14.10.'85
Dear Mr Griffiths
Re: NCB Houses for sale Llanharran

I am inquiring of the latest position regarding the above houses. Could you send me a list of houses currently up for sale as there are two members in St John's Colliery who continue to show interest? For instance is No 9 Westbourne Tce. Llanharan.
Many thanks for your previous co-operation.
Yours sincerely, Ian Isaac, Lodge Secretary

All the time there was still the day-to-day work of being a lodge secretary accountable to the lodge committee and the men, as well as providing a service for the public in respect of advice, information and support in applying for concessionary fuel, pensions and many social and economic issues of concern to people.

Some would call in for a chat and to pay their annual limited membership dues of 52p per year (1p a week). The NUM meant something to them. It was part of the fabric of the community. Below are some examples of the matters dealt with on a day-to-day basis:

Concessionary fuel
- Mr. Young, Turberville St. DOB 11/5/12 " Council will inform of change to Gas at his house in April 1985"
- Daniel V Healy, Lansbury Crescent:
  A hand written note from Idwal Isaac my father: "This man, an ex-miner called at the Lodge office today requesting information as to the procedure for helping his mother, the widow, for claiming for death benefit etc.
  The son living in Bridgend gave his phone number...
  Please give him a ring – his mother is too ill to deal with problems herself." Idwal.
  "PS. Owain has injured his toe - it is septic – it requires attention".

Housecoal:
- C W Tidball, Request for Quasi-Householder.
  Process to Ystrad Mynach
  As with much of my correspondence and notes in my archive it is marked with a large tick to indicate that it has been dealt with.

Accidents:
- Robert Phillips accident March 30, 1985 – took details of potential claim.

Most compensation work by then (from 1982) was being carried out by Phil White who would take down the details of any case and process them through the NUM's compensation system. We would claim significant amounts of money for injured miners and I recall reported more than £100,000 a year in successful claims being reported to the St John's Lodge NUM annual meeting. Phil and I always had a good understanding about the division of labour required to run an effective organisation and to raise the profile of the lodge and pit to prepare for the inevitable struggle to keep jobs in mining.

Family support vital

During the strike both my parents and my wife Jackie's parents did more than help out – the two boys virtually lived at their grandparents, often only coming home to sleep, ready for school in the mornings during the week. I would always try to be there to make breakfast and see the boys, Owain and Jason off to school in the mornings. I owe an enormous debt of gratitude to the children's grandparents they took the strain without question or reward. So, to Anita and John Jenkins and to Betty and Idwal Isaac, I shall always appreciate their selfless ways and what they did.

In memoriam: My mother Betty died in 1993 and a few years later, in 1997, my mother-in-law Anita died. They will be sadly missed by their children and grandchildren who witnessed their quiet yet important contribution that allowed me to play my part in the miners' strike.

The fight continues at area level

I attended the executive council of the South Wales NUM once a fortnight and confess to feeling that we, the lodge, were on our own for the most part. The NEC had ownership of the case once it was submitted to the Modified Coal Review Procedure. There were some officials more concerned about their power to make decisions than pursuing a case like St John's Colliery.

Minutes of Area Executive Council meeting held on Tuesday, September 24, 1985.

Matters Arising: St John's Colliery (See min No 355): *The area vice-president (Terry Thomas) inquired as to who invited Dr Andrew Glyn* [the Oxford Economist] *to the St John's Colliery review meeting, and also inquired as to why the executive was not informed that he was to attend.*

An explanation was given by an executive council member [it could only have been me - the minute taking was becoming more impersonal and in the third person] *for the Maesteg district that Dr Glyn had been invited by Dave Feickert, NUM National Research Officer.*

I made a note on the minutes as I had been in attendance: "Disagreement over involvement of Andrew Glyn – I made it clear that St John's NUM Lodge had no objection to his attendance. All experts were welcome to save our pit. While permission is welcomed - forget the niceties of permission from the executive council. There were men's jobs at stake". It was clear that because Andrew was a friend of mine his credentials were being challenged.

A local owner of a small mine makes life difficult

Report of National Executive Council Meeting held on Thursday, September 12, 1985, by George Rees, NEC member.

It was unfortunate that a local small mine owner had used the strike to run down his business and to sack two of his miners. We continued to do the best we could to represent them:

Bryn Newydd Licensed Mine: See Min No 372

"The area vice–president reported that he had sent a letter by "recorded delivery" to Mr. Rhys Jeffries, the owner of the above small mine, but he had received no reply. An executive member for the Maesteg District reported that both victimized men are suffering continual difficulties and that they were seeking further guidance.

"The area vice-president counseled that no decision should be made until further pressure had been brought to bear on Rhys Jeffries to re-employ them.

It was resolved to accept this advice and to bring the plight of the two men to the notice of the Finance and organisation sub-committee for its consideration."

10 November 1985: The election for South Wales Miners' President

EMLYN WILLIAMS announced his retirement for the end of 1985, nine months after the miners' strike and the campaign to elect a new president started. I was still quite young at 33 to consider standing for president. Had the industry been in a so-called normal state I probably wouldn't have stood. But I owed it to the rank and file who supported the Miners' Broad Left to provide an alternative to the former Communist leadership, and those area officials who were turning away from radical solutions to defend the mining industry.

From day one, this was to be massive ask for me to stand for president. In the ballot for president - for which I want to acknowledge the magnificent support of my lodge and supporters at St John's NUM - most of my second-preference votes went to Des Dutfield resulting in Terry Thomas, the then vice-president of the South Wales NUM, failing in his bid to become president.

I had 26 per cent of the first-preference votes cast, which I considered at the time to be a significant result and an affirmation of our ideas within the miners Broad Left which included active rank-and-file miners, Militant and the Labour Party Young Socialists in the coalfield.

Rank-and-file candidate

My decision to stand was made because it was felt by my friends and supporters that there was a need to provide a candidate for the active rank and file who had demonstrated exceptional resolve during the strike particularly those around the Miners Broad Left. I believed they deserved a new Left leadership at a time when the executive council in South Wales were distancing themselves from Arthur Scargill and becoming part of the new realist campaign of accommodation with the NCB and so-called market conditions.

Had Terry Thomas allied himself to those progressive elements within the coalfield around the new Miners' Broad left then I believe he would have become South Wales Miners president, such was the heightened political and trade union consciousness prevailing in South Wales after the strike.

These newly radicalised miners went back to work bloodied but unbowed.

There were ferocious arguments between the rank and file and those lodge officers that called for the status quo, keep your heads down hoping for better times and wanting to keep the lid on campaigning and lobbying for continued support against pit closures.

On reflection, Terry would have been a better president. He was more able, thoughtful and skilful in union negotiations than Des, who didn't have the negotiating experience of Terry, who had been a miners' agent for the Maesteg and Swansea District of the South Wales NUM since 1979. [The Maesteg and Swansea District covered pits from Cwm Colliery and Coedely in the East to Abernant, Bettws and Cynheidre Colliery in the West - some 18 lodges in all, the majority of the coalfield by then!]

Emlyn Williams the outgoing president was meant to have retired at the time of the strike – such is fate. He was one of the most able and inspirational orators I have ever heard. As a young miner I was spellbound by his ease of delivery of a case. I never failed but to support him. I learnt from him and I must say that he supported me too, but did so quietly behind the scenes. He never put an obstacle or any impediment in my way, but I had to fight my own corner on the South Wales Miners Executive, which I did despite considerable opposition on times from the officers, though rarely, I must add from the executive council members themselves.

I stood in that election and received 26 per cent of the first-preference votes in a pithead ballot vote using a single transferable voting system adopted by the NUM many years previously. The majority of second-preference votes on my first preference votes ballot sheets went to Des Dutfield. In other words those who had voted for me more then voted for Des Dutfield as a second preference than they did Terry Thomas.

Interference from the area office

In that election I experienced as much hostility from the established officers of the South Wales NUM as I did from the colliery manager in his attempts to close the pit. Area full-time officials had vetoed my election address in October 1985, demanding I delete any reference to my election slogan which was A Miners' President on a Miner's wage', along with doing everything they could to prevent me standing for area president.

My only ambition had only ever been to serve the NUM membership. This was clearly the last opportunity that I would have to represent those brave rank-and-file miners who saw the strike through for nearly a year and who continued to fight against pit closures. I explained in my election material that rather than drawing a full-time official's wage, which by then was nearly double that of a face worker, I would take only the average of a face worker and put the rest into a president's fund to help former miners and miners who experienced hardship.

IAN ISAAC
FOR PRESIDENT

A MINER'S PRESIDENT—ON A MINER'S WAGE
(Drawing the average wage of a face worker)

He has been an energetic Trade Unionist for many years.

IAN STANDS FOR :

★ A democratic Union built on confidence with the rank and file.

★ Membership involvement against rundown of our industry. Encourage every member to be an organiser in defence of his Industry and Union.

★ Getting the resources back to the Lodges.

★ Retirement at the age of 50 with dignity and average wage till 65.

★ A campaign for return of a LABOUR government committed to a Socialist expansion of the economy, restoring the manufacturing base—with full utilisation of coal products.

★ Adequate investments in each Pit, not just the few.

★ Regular consultation with men and Lodges with rallies and forums for the members to keep abreast of problems and issues.

★ Decent wage rates for miners comparable with highest paid industrial workers.

IF ELECTED, HE WILL :

★ Demand a major independent geological survey of all South Wales pits and reserves.

★ Explain in detail the internal accounting system for each Pit and Unit thereby providing men and Lodges with a platform to challenge the NCB on their own terms. A plan for each Pit and Workshop.

★ Encourage a major campaign of restoring membership confidence and build the democratic strength of the NUM to fend off attacks from the NCB and breakaway organisations.

Published by St John's Lodge NUM, Bangor Terrace, Nantyffyllon, Maesteg and Printed by Gibbs Bros. (Printers) Ltd. (TU), 14 Cross Street, Maesteg.

NUM (South Wales Area)
BALLOT FOR AREA PRESIDENT

VOTE FOR
IAN ISAAC
A MINERS' PRESIDENT
ON A MINER'S WAGE

"You can't do that!" shouted certain individuals, "that undermines the status of the position of president!"

However, I believed it would enhance the status of the president in the eyes of the ordinary miner, who received half the wages of the man who was supposed to be representing them. To be paid over the odds for the privilege of representing miners wasn't my idea of fair and equitable representation.

The resultant closure of virtually all the remaining pits in the South Wales Coalfield in a five-year period after the strike subsequently undermined the "status" of president, general secretary, research officer and many others who had "represented" the NUM.

It was clear to me that any obstacle thrown in my path would have to be dealt with. The prospect of becoming president of the South Wales Miners was a prize worth campaigning for because of the support I had been given by hundreds of rank-and-file miners before and during the 1984-85 strike. The irony was that I was also conducting the campaign as a platform of defiance against St John's Colliery being closed. By the time the campaign and election actually took place the pit was still being campaigned to be saved.

Did the industry collapse because the miners were too militant?

Between 1985 and 1990 The South Wales Miners Executive Council and its full-time officers witnessed the decimation of the South Wales coalfield. Was it their fault for being too defiant - because they were not? Did the pits continue to close because at last, in 1986 the Welsh miners had a reasonable moderate leadership? Who listened to their appeals for fair play and justice?

There is an old saying we used in the movement, "weakness invites aggression". The Government drove home their advantage at the invitation of moderation, appeasement and deference on the part of leaders in the trade union and Labour movement.

I often wonder what those miners in the Midlands who joined the breakaway Union of Democratic Miners (UDM), and who lost the vast majority of their jobs in the 1990s, thought of their right wing/moderate leadership when their pits closed.

These UDM men under their president Roy Lynk had been the compromisers and had been set up with state aid and succour to undermine the NUM. Did they lose their jobs because their leaders were 'too militant'? Because most of the time they were actually the opposite and were too moderate and wheeling and dealing.

I had always thought that it gave more dignity to have fought and lost than not to have fought at all. One constant strategy prevailed during that period - Margaret Thatcher's Government's policy to run down and privatise the high producing rump of the mining industry. Claude Von Clauswitz in his book On War said that "war was an extension of policy by other means". Thatcher and her advisers knew this as they embarked on their battles with the unions.

There were constant attempts to prevent me campaigning for the principles I felt were valid in the membership's eyes. General secretary George Rees wrote to insist that I delete parts of my election address in a further election in 1986.

My experience at having to blank out any reference to "**a miners' president on a miner's wage**" in this post-strike election was part of trend of interference from within, in the democratic process of trade union elections. This was another example of how the great democrats now operated after the strike who had achieved their positions through the campaigning of the old Communist-led "Left" in the NUM.

George Rees wrote to me on another occasion of my standing for the executive council triennial elections on December 4, 1986: "With regard to the leaflet you submitted to me for distribution in support of your campaign, I would inform you that the contents of the leaflet were not in order and I herewith enclose a copy of the leaflet which I would be pleased if you would amend before printing."

There were two demands starred or marked for deleting:"

* 1'(3) Against the imposition of having to buy back pension credits lost due to industrial disputes. He (Ian Isaac) is in favour of a non-contributory pension scheme. Already the miners' pension scheme is among the top 10 wealthiest schemes in the country. It should be phased in free for miners so that on leaving the industry after the age of 50 that they leave on the same level of lump sum and weekly benefits as the current Government-sponsored redundancy scheme."

Such censorship is used by trade union leaders with inappropriate power within the union structure. Whatever the merits of the demand, does it not make sense not to censor a person's views? Surely if the demands were outrageous or contravened rules then the members would decide whether they were appropriate or not.

*2 'He stands for: * Miners' Leaders on Miner's Wages plus necessary expenses for doing the job'.

While tactically removing the references or face disqualification, I continued to campaign for the principles I felt were right within the coalfield despite such bureaucratic interference.

11 The final act: Consulting the men about continuing the fight

On November 26, 1985, I convened a mass meeting of the membership at the Nantyffyllon Miners' Institute. This had been the fourth mass meeting since the end of the strike. We had always convened mass meetings to keep the members informed. The lodge remained defiant and at the invitation of the chairman, Charlie White, I presented the lodge recommendation to the meeting. I mustered every argument I could. There was a minimum of ten years and more work left in the mine.

We still campaigned for a new mine at Margam (near Aberbaiden) that potentially could be linked in to St John's. By now we knew as much as anyone about mining engineering, geology, the systems required to operate a mine and the best ways to manage a workforce and a mine.

We had made it our business to be as knowledgeable as the NCB and its managers and engineers in order to identify the truth to the question: "Were there sufficient winnable reserves in St John's to keep the mine open with an economic and viable return?'.

The answer was by then simple. It was **YES**.

The industry, St John's Colliery included, was being sacrificed at the political altar of the Tory Party. The NUM was the "brigade of guards" of the union movement. The aim of Prime Minister Margaret Thatcher was to use the state, including the judiciary and its armed forces to crush the miners' union.

So, the vote was taken: 109 for, 153 against. We didn't count the abstentions. A simple majority of 44 against the lodge recommendation to fight to keep the pit open and go through the Modified Colliery Review procedure. We therefore undertook to abide by the democratic decision of the members.

The lodge committee and its officers, having consulted the members through democratic means, would now inform the colliery manager that he could close the mine. We would offer whatever co-operation he required to process those who wished to take up redundancy and those who wished to transfer to receiving collieries which had posts to fill. Every man would be accommodated in accordance with his wishes.

I continued to represent the best interests of the men and made myself available to every interview for redundancy and to ensure that lists were drawn up for men requiring transfer. There were only 120 men wanting redundancy - all the remainder wanted transfer.

Buses were organised so that men could visit the 'receiving pits' to sign on. I recall Phil White, lodge compensation secretary and a fully qualified electrician, boarded a bus to the local Washeries only to be told that there was no job for him. He came back and I said: "It's best for you to just board a bus they have marked your card'. He and I were being blacklisted.

He boarded a bus for Abernant without his name being on the list. He was taken on as an electrician. They must have been in need of electricians at Abernant at the time. Phil White himself could tell the tale of how the industry continued to be run down as he went from pit to pit finally ending up in the last pit in the area.

Having kept a low profile for a few months, Phil later that year in 1986 was elected compensation secretary - a post he retained until a further transfer a year later to Tower Colliery. Phil became chairman of Tower Colliery NUM, a post he held until the pit closed in 1993. He was then secretary of the leadership team in the Tower Employee Buy Out (TEBO) that drafted the business plan and was chief negotiator with Government officials that had led to the TEBO.

Lodge chairman Charlie White takes ill

Before the colliery finally closed, Charlie White was taken ill. I have often wondered whether the pressure and stress of being, along with myself, at the forefront of the campaign to keep the pit open may have taken its toll on his health.

To outward appearances, Charlie looked a picture of health. He was naturally athletic and strong. Charlie had taken to wearing old suits to work in the last few months of the pit's life. It was his sense of defiance. They soon became unrecognisable as suits – looking more like smart black overalls with collars.

We were starting to be treated with a lack of respect by the colliery manager. If we didn't provide proof of being 'signed in' to work underground by the pit overman of the day then we would not be paid.

It had been custom and practice that the chairman and secretary would spend some time together discussing the issues of the day in the mornings after the men had descended to work underground. We would go over any issues, claims and requests by the men. The manager stated that if we were not underground by 7am then we wouldn't be paid.

In one of the final meetings at the pit, miners' agent Terry Thomas attended and informed the manager that unless the secretary and chairman received their wages for shifts that had been cropped from their pay packets, that he would refuse to conduct any further business with the manager under the conciliation agreement.

Later in the year I was with Charlie in his house before we had voted not to contest the closure of the pit on November 22, 1985. He was pacing up and down in his living room, saying: "they won't make us close our own colliery". Charlie wasn't well at the time and a few weeks later he died unexpectedly of a brain haemorrhage, an apparently hereditary condition that might have been treated had he had the results of tests sooner.

Charlie's funeral was one of the largest funerals I have ever attended. The family asked me to say the biding prayers and to give the tribute in the local Catholic church to Charlie's life, which in the previous eight years had been underground among the miners and active in the NUM.

It was a day of torrential rain. Charlie's brother was a Roman Catholic priest from London and he asked me to sit in the hearse with him, which I did, with his other brother in the back seat. As we approached the bridge over the old railway line that leads to Maesteg

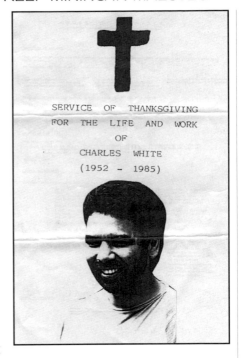

SERVICE OF THANKSGIVING FOR THE LIFE AND WORK OF CHARLES WHITE (1952 – 1985)

Cemetery a team of men stopped the hearse unfolded the Joint Lodges' banner and the bearers carried the coffin in the pouring rain behind the banner for more than half a mile up a steep slope to the cemetery.

We gave Charlie the best send-off we could. The white shirts of miners in the Crown Hotel after the funeral were steaming themselves dry from those who had endured the pouring rain to pay respect to Charlie White and his wife and sons. We had paid our respects as best we could in the tradition of the St. John's National Union of Miners Lodge, South Wales Area.

The pit closes and becomes history - winding up the affairs of the Lodge

St John's Colliery finally closed on 20 December, the day when the pit shut for Christmas in 1985. Officially the NCB records state November 1985. But then who is going to argue about a month? It was another case of 'to the victor the spoils'. They write their own history.

A crew of 20 or so men were kept on to salvage the pit. Lorry after lorry tipped aggregate (stones of various sizes) down the two shafts in order to create a seal and prevent the shafts collapsing. It took until March 1986 to complete the task. Ron Roberts the vice-chairman of the lodge stayed to the end in April 1985.

We continued to meet as a lodge until all the affairs were wound up in June 1986. My dealings with the general secretary of the South Wales NUM, however, were getting more and more difficult over returns of money due to the Lodge to settle its final affairs.

It was decided to hold a final lodge dinner and presentation and provide every member over the age of 50 with a miners' lamp in recognition of their services rendered. It was a tradition for men retiring from the industry to be acknowledged in this way. Men transferring to other pits were continuing with their service in the industry.

In the event, any monies left over were retained by the area NUM under rule. It left a bitter taste to be treated in such a bureaucratic way by your own area officials in the aftermath of the pit closing.

Transfer to a methane drainage plant.

During this time, I had taken up my new post with the NCB at their methane drainage plant at Abergwnyfi. I was just 400 yards away from the school I attended from the age of eight.

Attempts to transfer to another coalmine were prevented by a combination of NUM lodges and the NCB ensuring no place being provided for me despite repeated requests. I continued with my trade union activities as a member of the NUM and become a member of the Llynfi Valley Artisans Lodge, which had been newly formed by Terry Thomas the miners' agent to merge with what was left of the Tondu Artisans Lodge and the Maesteg Washeries.

I was also still representing the district as an executive council member and attended the merger meeting in that capacity. David Richards from the Maesteg Washeries was appointed by a show of hands as lodge secretary and Idris Rees elected chairman. They both did a good job representing the men for the remaining 10 years that the Washeries were open. I was reminded by Terry Thomas, that on the day of the merger I was still a member of the St John's NUM Lodge, which had not as then been officially wound up.

The end of an era!

The strike had been an eventful year for thousands of miners and their families. The year after was just as eventful for the miners of St John's. We had retained our dignity of purpose throughout. We continued to do our duty in representing the best interests of mineworkers, both at the pit and in the wider society.

We looked over our shoulder more than once to see if we really did have the support of the community and the Labour and trade union movement. Though many sympathised with our plight, there were individuals who took a cynical view, which was part of the media propaganda, that the pits closed because the miners were too militant!

The rundown of the British mining industry had been part of a political strategy on the part of the British ruling class. Margaret Thatcher, Nicholas Ridley, Peter Walker and Ian MacGregor were the instruments and the personification of that strategy. The details had been worked out by the various government agencies and intelligence services.

For so long as the institutions, trade unions and political parties claiming to represent ordinary working people of this country and internationally, fail to address the fundamental question of the fair and equitable distribution of wealth, and fail to run the various agencies of society on democratic lines, then there will always be rationalisations and rundowns in all industries and institutions until such time as alternative social and political structures representing the interests of working people are created. The failure to invest in labour, the communities where labour is produced and nurtured, and failure to invest in industry itself, leads to crisis after crisis.

12 1986 to 1989: three years in a methane drainage plant

My exile and reward for service to the NCB

My first day at the methane drainage plant in Blaengwnyfi was a combination of bewilderment and a sense of a new challenge. I recall looking around at the valley which was familiar to me because I had attended Abergwnyfi Primary School as a boy. The school had been demolished some years before but there was still the unmistakable dominant mountain that rose steeply from the road up to what was the school sports field, soccer pitch and venue for local football matches. It had been the venue for a scene in the film Blue Scar (1949), which featured a number of locations in the Afan and Llynfi Valleys. The film written and directed by Jill Craigie was a ninety minute drama about the Nationalisation of the coal industry in 1947. Locally miners remember one of the scenes in the film was of miners using Coegnant pithead baths. The cinema in Port Talbot was used as a makeshift studio.

I had carried out my exit duties at St John's and continued to be secretary of the lodge as we went through the final phase of winding up its affairs.

We used to meet in the lounge of the Riverboat Club in Caerau on Sunday mornings. Des Martin (brown boots) a former miner and his wife were the steward and stewardess. Des a former committeeman gave all the hospitality we needed free of charge a fact we appreciated at the time for about six months. I had vacated my office at Nantyffyllon Miners 'Library due to them redecorating the building and continued to be a trustee. (a short paper describing the history of North Memorial Halls is available from Afan Argoed)

I was to spend three years at the plant which was surrounded by a 14ft perimeter fence. Me, Derek Cole and Vic Robinson covered the plant 24 hours a day, seven days a week, 365 days a year. I continued with my trade union and Labour activity. I had an agreement with Derek and Vic that I didn't want to cover their shifts when they were on holidays they were to do that between them. I was only available to cover my seven days and any additional shifts that they couldn't cover themselves. I had a good working relationship with them both.

They were living locally in the village, and I travelled the eleven miles everyday either mornings 6am or afternoons 1.30pm, or nightshift 9.30 pm. We used to arrive early so that whoever was on shift was able to finish early.

Operating the plant

The basic operation involved was taking the barometer reading every shift, making sure that methane was drawn from the old workings at Afan Ocean Colliery and distributed via pipe network to Blaenant pithead baths, Cwm Coke works, and a plastics factory in the Garw valley, which was sited on an old colliery.

My job was to watch the dials and adjust the vacuums and pressures within the pumping arrangements in a large brick building. Our base was a converted caravan with all mod cons - a telephone (which I made good use of) a TV (for the quiet nights and the occasional sporting event) an electric fire (it could get cold on that exposed piece of ground in winter) a sink, a kettle and a microwave oven (home from home really!).

I played my part in organising the **re-elect Arthur Scargill** campaign from that methane drainage plant. I had been isolated from my rank-and-file contacts and I had been prevented from going to another colliery by the strategic decision of Cliff J Davies the NCB director with the collusion of NUM lodge leaders who had their own reasons for not supporting my transfer to their collieries at Blaenant and Bettws new mine.

The plant became my office

The plant became an ideal base from which to continue my trade union and Labour interests, even though I wasn't in daily physical contact with miners I could organise to meet them through the Miners' Broad Left and other organisations. I had my own typewriter, note pads and use of a telephone, and my newspapers. What more did I need?

In the summer of 1986, I was invited by the youth wing of PSOE - the Spanish Socialist Party, the equivalent of the Labour Party in the 1980s - to visit Asturias in northern Spain, which still had 20 coal mines in operation.

Miners there were experiencing the same political campaign from their government and the European Union to reduce coal mining capacity through a non-existent energy policy.

I used the plant's facilities to organise the trip. On arrival in Oviedo via Madrid, I spoke to the Spanish press and answered the following questions:

What's the reason for your trip to Austurias?

Answer: As a miner, a former local community councilor and sympathiser of the Marxist Left in the Labour Party I have been invited by the newspaper Nuevo Claridad, whose views I support, and to meet leaders of the trade unions in the mines in the Oviedo area; to learn as much as possible about the situation in the 20 or so Austurias coal mines which are currently under attack from the European Union and the Spanish government, threatening pit closures.

The Asturian miners sent support and money to the British miners during their year-long strike. Adrian Bird a miner from England had been out to the area during the strike and addressed meetings of the three main Spanish unions: PSOE, UGT, the Communist Workers Commissions and the small Catholic Workers' Union.

Food and money was sent back on many occasions during 1984/85. It is to offer to repay that debt of gratitude by being ready and armed with the feelings of the Spanish miners, together with the facts and figures to support them in their forthcoming struggle to defend their jobs. Even though this may take a different form to the British strike, like the recent three-day general strike in support of the miners, we want to be able to be of assistance and help their cause.

When asked what is the difference between Spain and Wales in terms of trade unions I replied: *"Miners are the same the world over... the slight differences there are, are to do with negotiation rights. In Spain you have three unions organising miners, whereas in the UK there is the one [the NUM, although by that time the UDM had been formed with Government money and backing)... but as witnessed in the recent dispute in Martsacro, the awareness of the threat to communities is the same. They acted as one." [The strikes in Spain were over job losses and pit closures. The same battle as we had experienced in the UK]*

After the long strike in the UK, what are the lessons?

"The need for Unity is imperative to work with other trade unions to agree a collaborative strategy of support and joint action where achievable. The miners cannot win on their own. I was impressed during the miners' strike at the willingness of ordinary people to come to the support of the miners."

I was then taken to a colliery at 6am in the morning and met with various union leaders in the lamp room. I was kitted out with a lamp and couldn't wait for my first visit to a Spanish coalmine. I was all set to go, when an official from PSOE advised us that everyone from 7am on that morning was now on strike, the decision taken that morning in the regional office of PSOE. I was disappointed but also pleased that action was being taken. I had to walk everywhere from a village called Mieres Blancas (White Stones) to various towns in the area. The miners had blocked the small towns and villages with telegraph poles to prevent commercial vehicles from delivering to the mines and the villages. All bar food and essentials was blockaded. I spoke on the regional radio about the need for solidarity against pit closures and was interviewed for the regional newspaper. For two weeks I was involved in a significant campaign which culminated in a mass rally supporting the miners in Oviedo, a city similar in size to Cardiff.

The whole terrain around Asturias is similar in geography to South Wales, with steep mountains and valleys and rolling hills and heath land. I witnessed miners walking home from shift wearing 'madrinas' which were like boots with cork studs.

similar to the old type of rugby boots worn after the Second World War up to the 1960s in Britain.

My experience in Asturias proved to me that miners were the same across the world. I also had met a woman miner, because legislation allowed women to have equal rights in Spain. This wasn't the case in Britain, due to a very different histori-cal development of the coalfields where exploitation of women and children was rife in the British coalfields of the 19th Century.

I had witnessed the capacity of the Spanish miners' unions to work together to bring the region to a halt. Nothing moved in or out of those valley towns for a week while I was there. I had to walk everywhere or at least walk from the outside of towns into the venues where I was to meet with miners, their families and their represen-tatives.

For a week my routine was as follows: Wake early and have a breakfast of hot chocolate and Madeira cake. Meet with young miners and political supporters and students in a local café. Meet with local groups and organisations at lunch. Have lunch typically a kind of Spanish 'broth' or 'cawl' with black pudding.

I would then travel to the venue for an evening meeting in a town or village hall. With my interpreter ever a constant companion, I was looked after in a local village that had a strong history of resistance against General Franco's republican forces in the Spanish civil war. Many Catholic priests were on the side of the unions and the workers' political parties. The names on streets testify to this day of the heroic struggles in northern towns and villages.

Left: Ian With Meeting Poster and Right: With female miner, Asturias

13 Arthur Scargill stands by the principle of re-election of full-time officials

On January 22, 1988, a ballot took place for re-election of national president of the NUM. In 1987, Arthur Scargill had continued with a high-profile campaign in the media and among miners of defiance against British Coal's attempts to introduce a new conciliation agreement detrimental to the interests of the members, and further rundown of the mining industry under new British Coal chairman Robert Haslam.

Tower NUM lodge secretary Tyrone O'Sullivan makes a reference in his book Tower of Strength, published in 2001, to an election that he declares he easily defeated me in. Unfortunately, I feel that Tyrone's account is an attempt to rewrite what actually happened during the campaign to get Arthur Scargill re-elected.

Helping with Arthur Scargill's re-election campaign

I spoke with Arthur Scargill over the telephone from the methane drainage plant I had been transferred to in Abergwynfi, and helped organise the first visit of his campaign in Wales to the BBC studios in Cardiff, where he conducted a famous, masterly interview with BBC presenter Vincent Kane.

Kane was visibly shaken by the forceful arguments of Arthur Scargill in that interview and it made every miner that watched it feel a head taller and enthused to continue the campaign against pits closing.

I assured Arthur that the South Wales rank-and-file miners were, by now, far to the left of their leaders, more progressive in their views and more prepared to continue the fight against pit closures. I also assured him that I was confident that they would return a resounding vote in favour of re-electing him president, despite the South Wales NUM Executive's hostility towards him.

The South Wales NUM Executive, under President Des Dutfield, had decided not to nominate anyone for the position of national president. This had never happened before. The South Wales Miners Executive had always recommended a candidate for a national office, such as vice-president, president or general secretary.

A resounding affirmation of leadership

Many young miners from the rank-and-file Broad Left that had emerged during the strike began challenging the old Communist left and the non-political elements in the South Wales and British coalfields, much to annoyance of the old official left around Mick McGahey

The Left, which was the old alliance of the Communist Party and the odd Labour Left MP and trade union official, had by this time largely disintegrated into the dust of the struggle itself.

The young Miners' Broad Left across Britain consisted of Militant supporters and many independent, left-leaning, rank-and-file miners who were attempting to put a strategy forward to unite miners around a socialist campaign to retain the mining industry.

The Broad Left had organised a fourth and final meeting of the elect Arthur Scargill campaign in the lounge of Neath Rugby Football Club. Of the 30 or so miners (mainly lodge committeemen and rank-and-file activists) at the meeting, it was down to Tyrone O'Sullivan or me to be the symbolic chair of the Elect Arthur Scargill committee in Wales - the election Tyrone refers to in his book.

At this last meeting it was decided to elect an official chairman for the campaign - we had taken it in turns until that point.

I lost this election by one vote when four Llynfi Valley miners (working in Bettws Colliery and Abernant Colliery) who had been due to attend the meeting to support me had been stopped by police on the way to Neath via Briton Ferry having been involved in a minor road traffic accident.

There were 27 miners in the meeting from eight different lodges across the coalfield. (I still have in my possession the attendance register signed by everyone there, together with their addresses and telephone numbers - no emails in those days).

Such is fate. I only stood because many rank-and-file miners didn't know where Tyrone stood on many issues even though he came across as a socialist. To this day he retains his own favoured personal brand of socialism. He favoured his own personal response to most situations. However, Tyrone, in his book seems intent on making it sound like a major election – it wasn't anything of the kind, the post was symbolic after all to be used for press purposes only. This was a group of rank-and-file miners organised by myself and Tyrone [who in those days had not experienced his pit closing and the miners buyout campaign], and a few other NUM lodge officials who were attempting to oppose the nomination boycott of the NUM South Wales Area Executive Council and to make sure Arthur Scargill was re-elected.

Arthur had been vilified by the press, government and media for the stand he had made against the run down of the coalfields. How could we stand aside and see him left on his own?

Despite his flamboyance, I appreciated the stand taken by Tyrone O'Sullivan, as he, like the rest of us, was committed to ensuring we covered the whole of the coalfield with Arthur Scargill's campaign literature, along with phoning up key individuals to discuss the mood and ask for support at their pits and to promote the campaign and encourage voting for Arthur Scargill.

The differences over the election of chairman of the campaign in South Wales didn't affect the re-elect Arthur Scargill campaign in 1987 because, ultimately, we all wanted to see Arthur re-elected. It was also the last ad hoc 'elect Arthur Scargill' campaign meeting in any event.

Arthur wasn't required to stand under rule but he was determined to put himself before the members for re-election after the miners' strike to reassert his authority as national president in the very hostile environment of a Coal Board and the ruling class hell bent on finishing off the mining Industry and its unions for good.

The role of the South Wales NUM Executive

Arthur received over 64 per cent of the vote in South Wales that year, and was re-elected as NUM President.

The result across the UK was 54 per cent in Arthur's favour against John Walsh, a right-wing Yorkshire miner. One irony was that I had sat in the same compartment as Walsh on a train to London the week before the election and had a fairly convivial conversation about his remote prospects and about rugby league for most of the journey.

John Walsh had spent his previous evening at the personal invitation of Phil Bowen, secretary of Blaenant NUM Lodge, at Seven Sisters Rugby Club. The majority of Blaenant miners went on to support Arthur Scargill in the ballot, which revealed a huge gap of consciousness opening up between the old lodge leadership of Phil Bowen and Lyn Harper and the rank-and-file miners of their own pit.

This was a good result for the Miners' Broad Left considering the pernicious campaigning of the new realist leadership in the executive of the South Wales Miners led by newly elected president Des Dutfield, general secretary George Rees and research officer Kim Howells, who was soon to become MP for Pontypridd.

The South Wales NUM Executive had failed to nominate Arthur having made a complete right-wing turn after the election of Des Dutfield as president in November 1985. He had taken up office in January 1986.

A political closure programme from start to finish

The mining industry had been shut down for reasons of political dogma and Tory strategy. The lack of decisive support from the TUC and Labour Party reminds me of that post war poem, testimony and lament of Pastor Martin Niemoller of the

German Unitarian Church in the 1930s when Hitler came to power, when he said: *"When they came for us nobody listened. When they came for the Jews nobody helped the Jews, when they came for the Communists, nobody helped the Communists. When they came for the social democrats, nobody helped them. When they came for the trade unionists, nobody helped the trade unionists. When they came for me, there was no-one left to help me!"* [first published in a book by Martin Mayer, They thought they were free, 1955].

The phrase has been adapted over the years, but Niemoller himself preferred the version that listed the Communists and trade unionists.

In the run-up to the election for national president, I organised a public meeting in Maesteg Town Hall where more than 800 people attended - such was the continued appeal of Arthur Scargill and his socialist views. At least 200 of those were from the public.

The executive turn their backs on struggle

The South Wales Miners Executive had taken a turn to the right and was hoping for a return to normality in terms of their relationships with what was by now British Coal.

Such sentiments resulted from a lack of power to influence events. They felt impotent in the face of the onslaught of mining engineers and British Coal officials on the closure campaign trail.

Arthur Scargill never formally aligned himself with the new Miners' Broad Left and continued to align himself with the former Communists and lefts in Scotland and Yorkshire where he could. But many former communists and the 'left' distanced themselves from him by now in Scotland favouring the campaign for a Scottish Parliament promoted by the Scottish TUC. In England and Wales these former 'lefts' were favouring a rush to join new Labour under Neil Kinnock.

The watchword in the Labour Party was 'don't rock the boat' and adopt any policies away from the left towards the centre of British politics. The quest for 'power' itself was the policy of the New Labour campaign. These were obviously Arthur's old network of friends and supporters who held various positions in the area leaderships.

The difference between Arthur Scargill's position and the "New Realists" as they were called, was that he and the Miners' Broad Left and active rank-and-file realised there could be no return to normal relations until the threat of closing pits for political and economic reasons was lifted.

There was a belief among the Miners' Broad Left that if we didn't remain vigilant and campaign with every means at our disposal to fight the closure programme then it would be accelerated.

Des Dutfield South Wales NUM President, writing in 'The South Wales Miner', the official journal of the South Wales NUM by now edited by Kim Howells, in January 1988, lamenting the lack of power in the coalfield, said: *"The election for national president was an enormous distraction which has prevented movement on these vital questions".*

Referring to the questions of pit closures, wages, conciliation and disciplinary code he added: *"These matters have been seriously clouded by the attention generated by the NUM presidential election."* He went on to justify the decision of the South Wales NUM Executive **not to nominate a candidate** as a case of them…*"believing that to do so would condone the way in which the election has been called… which we believe is constitutionally wrong".*

Such a stance was similar to the position taken by the Labour Party during the miners' strike itself. Rule books and constitutions were more precious to certain union leaders than the struggle to defend the pits and communities from the most savage onslaught of international and multinational companies' interests in reducing the reliance of the British economy on coal and its by-products.

In the same article in the 'South Wales Miner', called 'New Year, Old Odds', he went on to complain about outside interference in the affairs of the South Wales NUM. *"This interference has already caused a number of our lodges to object not only to the involvement of outside organisations, but also to the unwarranted interference of other lodges in their internal business."*

This 'complaint' about so called 'interference' was never a reality. It was a figment of their imagination. National elections within the NUM and its forerunner the MFGB had always been conducted internally and played out in public from Mabon through to A J Cook, Horner, Gormley and Arthur Scargill. Such elections were public and of interest to the working class who comprised that public; in particular mining communities. The South Wales Miners' leaders were by then looking inward and became so insular as to be virtually paralyzed and unable to resist the destruction of the industry.

A challenge from below

Such paralysis and paranoia about so-called 'interference' was prevalent in the South Wales coalfield until the last pit was closed. Certain lodge leaders felt threatened by the active rank and file who had learned so much during the strike itself.

NUM lodge officers, including the Blaenant Lodge officials who were behind the complaint, had welcomed contact and support from the wider community, trade unions and political parties and groups before and during the strike. So, what had changed?

Although I was subject to such accusations from the Blaenant NUM Lodge leadership who wrote a letter of complaint against me to the South Wales Miners Executive,

I challenged the legitimacy of such a complaint. And after much local campaigning by Tudor Parsons and Meirion Evans - both on the NUM Blaenant Lodge Committee - it fizzled out after six months when the rank and file at the pit convinced Secretary Phil Bowen and Chairman Lyn Harper to withdraw their complaint.

However, before that point arrived, I had received a letter from George Rees General Secretary NUM South Wales area, regarding the complaint from Blaenant Lodge, dated March 11, 1988.

In the letter he said the Blaenant Lodge had stated that:

1. On Sunday 22 November, 1987, you [Ian Isaac] as the National Secretary of the BLOC *(Broad Left Organising Committee that covered all trade unions)* Organisation organised a meeting at the Neath Rugby Club.
2. They claimed that in a press article by yourself in the newspaper Militant, it is clear that organisations such as BLOC were prepared to organise themselves in the internal affairs of Blaenant Lodge.
3. The lodge therefore felt that this BLOC Organisation, which involves elected and non-elected members of other lodges and organisations, has no right to interfere in the in the internal affairs of the Blaenant Lodge or any other lodge.

I had never been secretary of BLOC, which was a UK-wide, all trade union network of workers involved in a number trade union broad lefts, the NUM Miners' Broad left was one of them. My role was amongst the miners and not as a national organiser of BLOC which organised across all trade unions. The claim was clearly an invention, of Lyn Harper and Phil Bowen. They had a reputation for being parochial in all their dealings with the colliery and the NUM itself. There were a number of rank-and-file miners who belonged to the Miners' Broad Left including craftsman's rep Meirion Evans and youth rep Tudor Parsons.

Tudor represented a new generation of radical young miners ready to challenge for leadership in the lodge and coalfield.

In the end, I received a letter from George Rees on October 14, 1988.

It stated: "Thank you for your letter of October 4 in relation to Rule 38. A copy has been sent to Blaenant Lodge… If they have decided not to pursue the issue to Disciplinary Committee, the whole matter is now put aside."

I had written back to say that "I would be grateful… if he, [George Rees]

would convey my thanks and appreciation to the Blaenant Lodge officers and committee for wisely dropping the contested complaints against me and to also thank the membership."

I added that "both the lodge and the membership have my assurance that while I have publicly defended the policies of the NUM on British Coal's attempts to close mines for reasons other than proven exhaustion, and that I supported the re-election of the national president; at no time have I ever attempted to interfere with the internal affairs of the Blaenant Lodge. Paramount in my thoughts has always been the unity of the miners in the NUM advocating opposition to the Government and the Coal Board's attacks on our industry and communities."

A lot of arguing for common sense took place in the Blaenant NUM Lodge and I appreciated the position taken by many rank-and-file miners and certain committeemen in achieving the withdrawal of what was obviously a spiteful complaint attempting to curtail my activities in the coalfield on the part of the lodge leaders at Blaenant.

**When will the 'New Realists' stand for re-election?
Will they lead Welsh miners to six-day working?**

George Rees, area general secretary, elected for life?

Terry Thomas, NUM agent for life?

Area President, Des Dutfield: Can he hang on until 1990?

Broad Left activists answer attacks

IN THE last few weeks, Broad Left activists and particularly, *Militant* supporters in the South Wales coalfield have been subjected to the most vicious smears and lies by the Tory press, unfortunately egged on, in some measure, by our own area leaders. IT IS TIME TO PUT THE RECORD STRAIGHT.

The National Miners' Broad Left, since the announcement of the NUM presidential campaign, unashamedly backed Arthur Scargill's re-election just as vocally as the Tory rags were prepared to back anybody, except Scargill. However, to say that 'outsiders' intervened in the election is a lie. *The Mineworker* is produced by NUM members and no individuals who are non-NUM took part in the organisation of the 'Re-elect Scargill campaign'. In no way can the Broad Left be described as 'outside interference'. Our supporters are ALL rank and file miners or branch/area officials.

OUTSIDE INVOLVEMENT?

Instead of making public attacks on individual rank and file miners who came together to support Arthur Scargill in his presidential campaign, why didn't the area leadership condemn the blatant interference and attempts to influence the ballot by two South Wales Labour MP's, Ray Powell and Allan Rogers? Both publicly demanded that a member of the South Wales area stand against Scargill. Powell went as far as summoning our officers to Parliament. It's a pity these two individuals weren't as vocal in their support of the South Wales area during the strike.

What is even worse is that the area leadership are launching their attacks on us through the same rotten Tory press that vilified us all the way through the strike and have used as many column inches as possible to smear Scargill and achieve the best possible result for Thatcher and the bosses.

THE REAL ISSUES

The attacks on militant miners by the area leadership are very unfortunate. These are a smokescreen for the real reasons why some in our union are vilifying us. The question has to be asked, why don't the area leadership back Scargill when there is widespread support for him amongst rank and file South Wales miners?

Why is the area leadership continuing to demand negotiations with the Board on six-day working?

The majority of South Wales miners are opposed to flexible working, as shown in strikes recently in Lady Windsor, Deep Navigation and Taff-Merthyr. The dozens of miners lobbying our area conference for Scargill's nomination clearly reflected the real mood of the coalfields. Are they next to be slandered by the area leadership?

REAL ENEMY

We must never forget that the real enemy is the Tory government and British Coal. We call on the leadership of our union to lead a united struggle to stop pit closures, defeat six day working and achieve better pay and conditions for all.

14 1987 Margam:The attempt to turn the clock back 100 years

BY 1987, some NUM officials, it seemed, were prepared to sell out the miners' dignity for a pocket full of temporary bonuses in exchange for a six-day working week and nine-day fortnight at the proposed Margam New Mine in 1987. Yes, it nearly happened!

In the name of moderation and appeasement, the South Wales NUM nearly sold out. Only by a rigorous campaign of defiance against their own union did the rank-and-file win the day and bury the six-day week and nine-day fortnight destined for the Margam New Mine. Me and Andrew Glyn had managed to get our material to all the lodges.

The opening of the new mine still hasn't gone ahead to this day, though there have been a number of attempts over the years. Either the markets haven't been right for grade 301, a coking coal (the best around), or the miners haven't been compliant enough!

Andrew Glyn a Fellow in Economics at Corpus Christi College, Oxford, and myself, organised a two-man campaign in the South Wales coalfield against six-day working. I had been a student of and a political and economic collaborator of Andrew Glyn when I lived in Oxford between 1969 and 1973, and again later in 1976 to 1978 when at Ruskin College and through to the miners' strike and after when collaborating in 1987 against the imposition of a six-day working week for miners in the proposed Margam new mine. He had been a friend and collaborator for over 30 years.

I like to think we made enough of a contribution among the rank-and-file miners to win the day. I was still working at the methane drainage plant in Abergwynfi. Andrew and I researched and wrote a thorough exposition of the six-day working fraud. Using the figures provided by the Coal Board, Andrew showed that the Margam New Mine was not cost effective on the basis of a six-day working agreement.

Andrew and some of his fellow Oxford academics have been an inspiration to me over the years. While I used academic research to promote our arguments it was the political and trade union principles that counted. I admired his straightforward approach to industry and the needs of ordinary working people. He was a gentleman and an advocate of the truth.

I recall myself, Andrew and Wendy Carlin, Andrew's wife, a distinguished Cambridge economist herself, meeting with a St John's Colliery clerk on a Saturday morning after we had returned to work after the strike, at a rendezvous near the pit to receive copies of all the costings and financial statements regarding St John's Colliery operations.

I shall for ever be in that colliery clerk's debt for providing such vital information that assisted our case against pit closures.

It was a brave thing to do to "blow the whistle" at that time. Had he been found out, he would have most certainly have lost his job. We were able to match this information with material we had obtained from the NCB Tondu headquarters in 1983 when miners broke into the local NCB HQ to obtain the Margam information and other sensitive material.

St John's was the first individual pit that Andrew studied, and we published our findings in pamphlet form and submitted then to the independent inquiry into the case for St John's Colliery the previous year. He continued with a number of studies for the NUM including pits earmarked for the new Modified Colliery Review procedure.

His work was quoted in the campaign to keep Polmaise Colliery and other Scottish pits open as well as others throughout the UK. Andrew died during Christmas 2007 after a life time of commitment to the trade union movement in Britain and internationally.

His CV read like an international commuter to universities from Oxford to Tokyo and to Harvard and more. He was a miners' supporter all his adult life.

I wrote to Wendy Carlin his widow expressing my sincerest condolences:

Wendy Carlin/Glyn
Oxford
8 January, 2008

Dear Wendy,
I have only today heard the news about Andrew's tragic death from Ken Smith via Lynn Walsh. They had told me via my work's email and I didn't get the message until I returned to work after the Christmas break. It is difficult to convey in words to you how much I respected him and his work over the past 35 years that I had known him.
I cannot begin to understand how you must still be feeling at such a huge personal loss to yourself and the family.
You may recall meeting me a few times during the 1980s and early 1990s when Andrew was working on one of his great passions which was the miners' cause and the state of the mining Industry which was so badly run and used by politicians, Labour

and Conservative alike, following Nationalisation. We of course do our own work and pursue our own passions. But every now and then you meet someone who has that touch of humanity. That was Andrew. He transferred that humanity into a highly technical subject such as economics can be.

When I was a student in Ruskin College in 1976, I set up a Marxist economics group. Six of us Ruskin Students met once a month in Corpus Christi under Andrew's guidance. I still have the complete works of Das Capital at home – I have an admission to make... I never read it all. Andrew said the first 100 pages are good. That was good enough for me. So I read them.

I first met Andrew in Merle and John's house in West Oxford in the early 1970s. I was a shop steward in E Block, Cowley, and I was fascinated by my acceptance by highly qualified people like Andrew, who was already well on his way to accomplishing a lifetime's work with his friends Phil Young and Bob Sutcliffe in the Economics Institute. We both wrote articles for Militant at the time.

When I moved back home to Wales it was during the miners' strike that I reconnected with Andrew, and he was so influential in my ability as Lodge secretary and executive council member to argue the miners' case against the pit closing locally in St John's Colliery, Maesteg.

We wrote an important pamphlet together that helped prevent jobs from being lost for nearly a year whilst we campaigned. It was called 'Keep Mining in Maesteg'. Andrew gave evidence at an independent inquiry in Cardiff into the issue of the St John's pit closing in 1985. The inquiry concluded that there was no case for closing the colliery. With experts like Andrew there could not have been any other outcome. What a giant when by your side. I was also always quoting from his pamphlet written for Arthur Scargill and the NUM and those he wrote for Neil Kinnock, then leader of the Labour Party. We also jointly wrote a paper opposing the introduction of six-day working in the mines of the South Wales Area. We won that one by the two of us campaigning, I like to think. Needless to say, despite the leadership of the South Wales NUM in 1989 being in favour of it, the Coal Board dropped the idea when they dropped the decision to reopen the Margam New Mine.

During the 1990s I worked for a national mental health charity as a regional development officer. Andrew paved the way for our national Development team, which I was a facilitator of, to meet at Corpus Christi College Oxford. The oak-paneled lecture rooms were a contrast to our normal offices and meeting rooms. He convinced the bursar that it was for a good cause. We were never charged a thing in the two years we used the facility.

In 2005, Andrew contacted me over an article he was writing for the 'Pelican' The Corpus Christi College annual publication, the article was reviewing the industry at the time of the 20th anniversary of the Miners' Strike. What a surprise and a sense of humility I had when he mentioned my name as his friend in the article.

I suspect that I am one of hundreds of people who have been touched by his brilliance. He kept urging me to finish a book I was writing on the Miners' Strike from a personal perspective. I used to tell him stories about it – he was ever the listener. When I finish it, I will with your permission, dedicate it to Andrew in honour of his commitment to the miners' cause.

Please forgive me for going on a bit, but I do so feel ashamed that I couldn't be at the funeral and to give my personal condolences to you.

If there is ever anything I can do to help you in any way or to preserve Andrew's legacy for all time please feel free to contact me.

My sincerest condolences.

Ian Isaac, a Friend

1986 was the end of an era for many South Wales mining valleys. Compare Andrew Glyn's analysis with that of George Rees and Des Dutfield in the 1984 to 1986 annual report submitted to the annual conference of the South Wales NUM below:

NUM South Wales Area Council, Annual Conference
Agenda and Annual Report for 1984-1986
Retirement of Mr Emlyn Williams

On 21 February 1986, Emlyn Williams, president since 1973, retired.
He was a tank commander during the war.
Emlyn found it impossible to disassociate mining trade unionism from politics.
He served on the Labour Party NEC
6,500 left the mining industry in Wales from February 1986 to May 1986 ibid
The union's chief administrative officer, Don Hayward retired through ill health. W D (Danny) Williams retired as compensation agent.

15 lodges, 14 collieries closed during that period. [The report then simply reads- my note II]... "the area executive council , area officials and staff would like to place on record their thanks and appreciation to the Lodge officers and committeemen of the following Lodges which have closed in the last 12 months:"

Bedwas; Treforgan; Vale of Neath; Tondu Artisans; Penrhiwceiber; Markham; Bleanserchan; Celynen South; Celynen North; Roseheyworth; Britannia; Ogmore Valley; Garw Valley; Coedely [Note St John's Colliery was omitted from the above list despite closing in December 1985. Perhaps St John's Lodge officials and committeemen didn't qualify for thanks and appreciation as lodge officers. Was it an oversight? – only those who wrote the report will know!]

In 1986 George Rees further wrote in the union's annual report:

"Coalmining will, in the medium term at least, be inextricably bound to the fate of manufacturing industries and to overall policies of Government intervention or non-intervention in determining the economic direction which those industries take. It follows that the NUM must make reciprocal moves to reflect through formal and informal alliances these more direct links forged by management between the supply and demand sides of the business.

"The isolationism and vanguardism which appeared to infect so many decisions made by the NUM during the strike owed a great deal to the onerous belief, rampant in certain quarters of the union, that it was not really a function of the NUM to acquaint itself with the realities of customer demand or with the wider economic implications of a deteriorating manufacturing base."

Had the South Wales NUM leadership acquainted itself with the realities of *"customer demand"*, then they would have realised that governments had manipulated the customer base for the past decade and more and more had refused to reinvest in manufacturing industries to compete in the world markets, along with a refusal to invest in research and development for alternative uses for coal, clean technologies for fluidised bed combustion in the power industry was deliberately underinvested, which resulted in government not the NUM national leadership ignoring the realities of customer demand.

The trend was a political trend away from coal for political reasons and not for pure market reasons. Was it the role of the NUM to negotiate agreements to assist in that downward trend or to stand up and demand respect for better wages and conditions and a continued fight against pit closures?

One further irony in that report above was that Des Dutfield (to be elected president of the South Wales NUM early in 1986) in a speech to a national NUM conference whilst still on strike on March 3, 1985, in TUC Congress House London, criticised the national leadership when referring to *"the [NUM] NEC not making recommendations."*

Nearly two years later, on the important occasion of a national election for NUM president, he too, as South Wales NUM president was refusing to make a recommendation in respect of who the South Wales Area should nominate and recommend in a ballot for national president.

Had Arthur Scargill received the nomination from the South Wales Miners' Executive *"to assess the situation where we were going democratically"* (Des Dutfield's words) there would, in my opinion, have been a further 10 to 15 per cent rise in the 64 per cent share of the vote in his favour. Men respect the opinions and recommendations of their elected leaders and they carry a lot of weight when it comes to who the rank and file eventually vote for in a ballot!

In 1988 Arthur Scargill took up his final tenure of office having been over 50 years of age and democratically re-elected by a comfortable majority of British mineworkers, despite the most vicious internal and external campaign of vilification against him and the Miners' Broad Left.

He never formally associated himself with the National Miners' Broad Left, maintaining tenuous contact with the former left of the Communist Party and area officials on the left of the Labour Party some of whom who were his life long acquaintances and supporters. His ideas were nevertheless more associated with the National Miners' Broad Left who supported him and published all their ideas during the strike.

The so-called Left didn't publish a single position formally as a forum of opinion throughout the strike or after. Everything was decided behind closed doors. The work of the Miners Broad Left was open, transparent and inclusive of the rank and file.

15 1989: The end of 15 years' involvement in the NUM and mining

After Arthur Scargill was re-elected national president in January 1988, I continued to maintain contact with the National Miners' Broad Left and attended various meetings nationally.

The following collieries closed during 1988: Abernant, Abercynon, Cynheidre, Marine, Six Bells, Merthyr Vale, Oakdale and Trelewis Drift.

In 1988, 40 collieries closed in the UK. The TUC capitulated to both the Tories and New Labour in supporting the interests of private wealth creation and big business was prepared behind the scenes to support the expulsion of union fighters from the Labour Party.

Neil Kinnock prepared the way for expulsions in his 1985/86 Bournemouth Labour Party conference speech, attacking the Militant-led Liverpool City Council in its stand against cutting expenditure, he denounced: "The hideous spectre of Labour councillors and officials going around in taxis delivering redundancy papers to council workers".

This was a publicity stunt orchestrated by Kinnock at the Labour Party Conference. But he didn't once complain when the Thatcher Government was refusing to release the funds to Liverpool City Council because they took a stand against cuts in services, which in themselves were going to result in redundancies. Had the council not issued the redundancy notices required under law they would have been sued.

When a government refuses to release the rate support grant what other course of action was there? To stand on the sidelines criticising the efforts of a left-wing council's attempts to build new homes and run better services became the custom of Labour leaders in the 1980s.

The situation was getting more difficult every month, with pits closing sometimes by default. In August 1988, the methane drainage plant was running out of methane extracted from the old colliery workings. We suspected a fall of ground around the large pipe that was walled in at the pit bottom thereby preventing air being drawn by the surface pumping station. The vacuum readings at the main methane drainage plant were getting dangerously high and could have led to an incident of implosion in the shaft or in the methane drainage plant itself.

The NCB therefore decided to shut down the operations and seal off the drainage systems from underground and make it all safe. To this day there is a small compound with a vent allowing any gas to go to atmosphere from the site itself.

Redundancy or leave!

All three operators, including myself, indicated that we would not take redundancy and opted to be transferred to Blaenant Colliery. We were interviewed by a Mr Joe Coyle from the industrial relations department,

For some reason the decision to allow transfer was proving difficult to carry out. I was told privately that Derek and Vic could transfer but there was no post for me. It was déjà vu all over again. I talked it over with my family and decided to make a stand and refuse redundancy seeking a transfer to another pit.

In October 1988, the weather was particularly bad for that time of year. Day after day was spent travelling to a deserted, non-functioning methane drainage plant. Three men in their separate shifts sitting in a caravan looking after a 14ft perimeter fence in a locked compound, the public were by now prevented from entering the compound, even though it had been completely sealed off for three months. The wind and rain were constant companions.

Lookouts for the NCB

On a few afternoon shifts when it became dark I took it upon myself (there were some pressing domestic issues at the time over childcare arrangements, and I couldn't afford the time off) to secure the compound and travel home. Little did I realise that security men from British Coal had been sent to spy on the comings and goings of the plant operators, or was it me? It was pointed out at a hearing to establish facts in the Maesteg Washeries, with my lodge secretary David 'Dai Gits' Richards, that security officers had compiled a report having observed the plant with binoculars for a period of time. I was caught in a trap.

I fought as hard as I could by explaining that the reason for leaving my post was due to family reasons. It was a minor indiscretion to say the least in the circumstances. I was the victim of a campaign to obtain evidence against me so that my transfer could be prevented. I was suspended on full pay until the matter was finally resolved at the 11th hour with a tribunal pending in February 1989.

Terry Thomas, the miners' agent, hosted and facilitated the negotiations between British Coal and their solicitor in Doncaster from his office in Swansea. My lodge secretary was present and after a day of negotiations it was finally agreed that I could be retained in employment in the mining industry in the Nottingham coalfield or except a lump sum payment equivalent to a year's pay. At 4.50pm on a Friday afternoon, I accepted the final offer of a year's pay in an out of court settlement; the details to be transcribed for the following Monday. We agreed that the tribunal would be informed.

The prospect of starting all over again in a strange coalfield was not appealing, given that my family was still young and I had been uprooted a few times during my childhood and didn't want to confer the same experience on my children. There can be times for martyrs and this wasn't such a time.

I had witnessed my last incident in the mining industry and from then on I would only observe the withering away of a once robust and dynamic industry where communities had been forged out of the human endeavour which brought together people from all over Wales and the West Country.

1994 – The last pit in Wales, miners buy their pit

The Tories, and the ruling elite of Great Britain, the state in its various forms, had decimated the mining industry in Wales, Scotland, Kent and North Wales and significantly reduced it in England

There was one deep mine pit left in Wales. There was some mining in slants and small mines, but by and large the industry had been destroyed.

Successive governments had failed to address the question of workers' management in the mining industry, preferring instead to have consultative machinery set up on colliery, area and national basis. These consultative committees did address safety, coal distribution and technical matters but rarely ventured into industrial relations. No legislation was brought forward to allow the miners to run their own industry until ironically the Act to Privatise British Coal and put the remaining pits out to tender for private ownership.

The Tower Employee Buy Out bid (TEBO) became the successful bid for Wales under the privatisation tendering process. Miners in South Wales had always been inventive in their approach to problem solving and this bid to run their own mine was an expression of those skills and abilities on the part of the only remaining lodge leadership in the South Wales Coalfield. Tower Colliery by then had men transferred in from Maesteg, Afan Valley, Swansea Valley and virtually every part of the coalfield.

The resulting form of governance involved the men holding shares to the value of £8,000, which they gave from their hard-earned wages and savings, electing representatives to their board and, ironically, inviting Phil Weekes to be their chairman of the Board. He was the former area boss for the Coal Board who had a reputation for being a knowledgeable mining engineer and a fair and honest man, though he did play a role in kick starting the miners' strike in Wales, then retiring a few months after the strike. It was he who announced the closure of six pits – including St John's Colliery in March 1984.

The fight to keep Tower Colliery open as the last deep mine in Wales in the 1990s was, ironically, made possible by the privatisation of the mining industry.

Michael Heseltine, by then time deputy prime minister, had had a love-hate relationship with the miners (South Staffordshire miners had dug a massive hole in his lawn and filled it with coal during their struggle to keep pits open).

When the Tower miners approached the bankers in the City of London and presented the TEBO bid, Tory cabinet minister Heseltine was ready to "forgive" the miners, (such is the political "expediency" from time to time of establishment politicians) and it was indeed an irony when he announced in Parliament in 1994 that the TEBO bid had been successful.

Phil White, a friend for most of my adult life was an employee director of the Tower Colliery responsible for marketing and distribution.

While Tyrone O'Sullivan continued as spokesman for Tower NUM during the campaign to buy the pit, Phil White as mentioned earlier, was secretary of TEBO working on the business plan and marketing, skills necessary to run a successful workers' company. Phil had been chairman of Tower NUM Lodge. He had been transferred from St John's Colliery to Abernant Colliery then Tower Colliery and could always see the bigger picture when others would live on past reputations and laments. Phil also played a key role as secretary of the national campaign to reinstate sacked miners from 1985 to 1987 called 'Justice for Mineworkers'.

It would have made no sense for Tower Colliery to be part of the Budge Mining Group bid which saw many collieries become part of a large private consortium run by Peter Budge in the Midlands and Northern coalfields.

In 2008, Tower Colliery closed due to reasons of proven exhaustion of coal - 14 years after a mine that had been declared uneconomic in 1994 was "closed". Just as the miners had argued for during the strike; the coal was there to be mined and at a profit. The Tower miners kept the pit open 14 years more than British Coal intended and are now the proud owners of acres of land capable of being redeveloped for economic and hopefully community regeneration in a former mining area on the slopes of the Rhigos Mountain.

The miners as shareholders now own hundreds of acres of industrial development land and I'm informed that they intend to redevelop the land in partnership with investment bodies. In any event they will have secured their future as the struggle had intended.

Tory MP and cabinet minister Nicholas Ridley had once pondered how his strategy might have broken up the mining industry in that long-forgotten paper he presented in 1978. Little did he realise that one of his options for "workers' co-operatives" as part of a mix of governance for mining coal in Britain would be enacted by the last deep mine in Wales in 1994.

A transition following 10 years of struggle

It took some time to adjust psychologically after I left the mining industry. Personally I missed it. I missed the camaraderie of miners and their role within the community. I missed it because of my family connections to mining for over 100 years, two of my great grandfathers on both sides of my family were working in the mines in 1880s in the Garw, Llynfi and Afan Valleys. One of the sons of those great-grandfathers settled in West Wales at Golden Grove where my mother was born.

I likened it to a psychological metamorphosis when a caterpillar sheds its skin to find a butterfly within. My life as a union official in the NUM was now something of the past. The future would have to be hewn out of material other than coal.

In July 1989, I obtained work as a Wales Development Officer for a mental health charity, helping to decommission the large psychiatric hospitals settling former long-term patients into the community and creating a community psychiatric care service involving the voluntary sector. I enjoyed the challenge of increasing the activity and project base of the organisation from £20,000 to a sum of £1.5 million with 25 staff employed when I left in the summer of 2000 by mutual agreement, having worked 11 years for them. The struggles to make things happen for the best interests of people and their carers who had experienced serious mental illness is another story, but one that I immensely enjoyed.

In October 1988, I was expelled from the Labour Party. This was a culmination of attacks upon me for the role I had played during the strike and afterwards, and for my association with Militant, before and during the strike.

Proceedings had begun in July 1986 after the colliery had closed. My barrister conducted a brilliant case in defence of my membership at a three-day hearing at Labour's HQ. I am still indebted to all those who gave money to the Ogmore campaign against expulsions. It was in a modern sense every bit a witch-hunt.

I produced a 200-page dossier in support of my case with testimony from over 50 people who were trade union activists and Labour Party members. All describe my role in the Miners Strike, The campaign for Jobs in Maesteg, and my continued campaign for justice for miners and others.

I rejoined the Labour Party in 1998, ten years later, without conceding any of my socialist principles or yielding to any of the spurious allegations made 10 years previously by a local gang of political hyenas desperate to get me out of their path to political office. However, it has been saddening to see the drift to the right by Labour in recent decades.

In April 2001, I started work with a community regeneration organisation in Sandfields, Aberavon, a South Wales community in Port Talbot suffering the neglect of successive governments over the previous 40 years. I am currently its chief executive, helping convert community buildings for community assets and facilities, helping create jobs, employing presently 25 staff in the recession of 2008/09. The organisation are involved in community engagement projects aimed at economically inactive people covering the Neath Port Talbot area and helping the local community develop skills and abilities to make a difference to the quality of life of people living in the area. I now help 'regenerate communities'.

Twenty-five years on and still the debates among former miners are to be heard in the coffee shops, street corners, living rooms, parlours and of course clubs and pubs.

I was a young miner in August 1974 having just missed the 1974 strike. By 1984 I had become wise to the forces at play in Britain at that time.

When miners warned: "When you shut a pit you kill a community" – no-one took us seriously. To this day we witness rates of economic inactivity at levels up to 60 per cent of the adult population of many former mining and industrial areas which have become Welsh Assembly Government-funded Communities First programme areas in Wales. I work for a community regeneration organisation that attempts to provide opportunities for people against a back drop of 58 per cent economic inactivity for people of working age. This is 25 years after the miners' strike and the subsequent rundown in manpower in the steel industry and manufacturing in the eastern and western valleys and coastal areas.

We also warned during the strike that when you close the pits and factories, communities would lose a significant amount of income and spending power that would help to nurture and bring up the next generation of young people – again not enough people listened. If they did they were unable to influence change even when New Labour came into Government in 1997.

The loss of opportunity for young apprentices, young men becoming mining trainees and well-rounded individuals taking their place in civil society if a university career wasn't their calling, has been lost.

My opinion is that a whole way of life has been sacrificed at the altar of privilege and greed. But we understood and learned where we were in this disfunctioning society based on the private ownership of the means of production. We live in a society divided into thirds in terms of social and economic terms: one-third extremely wealthy, one-third with incomes enabling house ownership and average living standards and one-third having incomes less than £12,000 a year or benefits that barely stave off poverty for themselves and their children.

That cannot be a comfort to those who have managed to get by and obtained well-paid jobs when so much child poverty still exists in the former mining communities in Wales.

We had warned as far back as 1986 (as had others before us) that the credit and economic "bubbles" would burst when finance houses and banks were lending as much as six times the combined annual income of young couples wanting to buy their own homes and offering further credit on store cards and credits cards. Such a way of living can never be sustainable.

There had been a slump in house prices in 1987/1992, but the "bubble" started all over again until the 2007/08 credit crunch fuelled by the sub-prime dealings in America and the UK banks and finance houses that bought into its parceling up of debt and the hedge funds that profited form it until the banking crises when they refused to lend to each other based on lack of trust in collateral. Now it is very hard indeed for young couples to buy their own houses. Lack of opportunities for advancement for young people will be a hallmark of this generation of young people as the so called 'loads of money' opportunities was for the last generation. My own son Owain experienced the Thatcher YTS (Youth Training Scheme) generation lack of opportunities in the 1980s.

The surplus value of world production is hoovered up in the form of hedge funds, private equity clubs and offshore funds which provide large management fees for transactions for financiers and large returns for investors, all one and more steps removed from the production of wealth in industry. There has been a parceling up of debt and increased speculating, in the form of private equity clubs leveraging debt out of large companies as 'going concerns' and passing the proceeds off as large percentage returns on investments to members of the private equity(investors) club. Warren Buffet the American billionaire personal wealth $40 billion is one example, but there are others in Britain who simply asset strip industry for private gain and dividends to investors.

(For insights and examples I would highly recommend Robert Peston's Who Runs Britain, published 2008 and Building Jerusalem by Tristram Hunt, another book that underpins the story of the battle between capital and labour in Britain from Victorian times to the present

The rundown in manufacturing, steel making and iron foundries within the British economy has left us without any claim to being the "workshop of the world". That mantle has passed to China.

The debate about reducing the amount of carbon in the world's atmosphere was always embraced by the Miners' Broad Left within the NUM. The worst thing in many ways you could do with coal was to burn it. It has so many other uses which would retain the carbon in an inert state for uses to improve the quality of life of people living in former mining communities.

For now the problem has been exported to China and India which burn poor quality coal in enormous quantities and where cheap local energy sources for industrial development are mined in unsafe dangerous mines and used in unsafe steelworks throughout China and Asia.

Until the world's decision-making forces grasp the nettle and embrace sustainable economic development within a growth-neutral philosophy, then we will continue to import goods and services funded by an economic growth based on burning coal without preventing the pollution of the world's atmosphere.

The owners and custodians of capital have no consciousness other than the uncontrolled accumulation of wealth, which they retain for reasons of financial speculation and not economic growth or to offer improvements to the quality of life and working and living environments of the world's population.

Their problem is that they don't know what to do with surplus value other than continue to place it in the money markets or make more wealth from acquisitions and mergers. That remains our problem because it is not possible for us to buy back all that we produce whether in goods or as added value in terms of goods, services and environments.

Fifteen years in the mining industry could have been a worthwhile investment and contribution to the quality of life in society. I hope that I have provided some insight for young community, trade union and political activists today to learn the lessons of the struggles and methods of organising of the past. This is so as not to repeat the same mistakes and not to have to travel the same path, but to develop their strategies and skills necessary to maintain the quality of life of people that they represent. The lessons I have learned during that time have stayed with me for the past 20 years since leaving it in 1989.

Postscript

I had written the essential parts of this account within five years of leaving the mining industry. I kept an extensive archive of press cuttings, minutes and hand-written material, other written material, cassette tapes and video tapes and I felt that to publish my recollections and appraisal of the period would have been premature.

If I had, it would have been filled with anger and a desire to hit back at society or individuals in a personal sense. I hope I have avoided that by surviving long enough to give a balanced view as well as a contemporary personal view of the events of that period. Leaving the account until now, on the 25th anniversary of the end of the miners' strike, allows, I hope, an instructive, rational and objective element that can be inserted while still allowing my subjective impressions to come through and play an important role in explaining the past.

To learn the lessons of that time will be instructive for future generations who may well have similar challenges to face in their daily lives. This book was written 24 years after one of the most momentous struggles in British trade union and Labour history. The actual 25th anniversary of the end of the dispute is March 5, 2010. The event, in terms of political, trade union, rank-and-file participation and organisation, ranks alongside, in its significance, with the General Strike of 1926, the campaigns against war on the Clyde in 1914-1918 and the Glasgow rent strikes of 1919-1920. (Further reading: William Gallacher, Revolt on the Clyde, Lawrence & Wishart)

No miner gave up a year of his working life for the sake of it. They did so consciously in the attempt to preserve the industry that they were part of and earned their living from. They did so to meet their immediate needs and in the hope that their sons, nephews and grandsons may have an option of a career in a great industry despite the latent problems associated with pneumoconiosis and many other dangers involved in the extractive process of coal production.

To mitigate the affects on the health of mineworkers, policies were fought for:

- To retire at 50 years of age and to introduce modern ventilation techniques and cleaner processes was promoted by the NUM.
- To have cleaner and innovative uses for coal besides burning it.

If this account has helped to raise awareness of the real issues at stake before during and after the miners' strike of 1984-85 then it will have achieved its aim. This is not meant to be a tabloid account where blame is levelled at one man or one union for the loss of a major industry in Britain.

It was clearly the stage where the respective forces of capital and labour rehearsed and fought for their diametrically opposed interests. It was a struggle for the hearts and minds of the rank-and-file and a test of who had the right mettle and credentials to lead them. This always takes place, but during the strike it was particularly intense. Every miner had a critical view of their leaders. The point was to get the leaders with the right policies and outlook using democratic means via the ballot box even for full-time paid officials.

There were far too many unelected appointments (key staff members) within the NUM at area and national level. There were as many as 12 unelected staff employed by the area union, including key positions during the strike such as finance officers, picketing organisers, and compensation officers. In the NUM HQ, it was clear that MI6 had people working for them. Roger Windsor, a non-elected chief executive officer is a case in point (see Seumas Milne's book The Enemy Within). Without doubt this practice of the state of planting people to work for them also took place in other NUM area HQs. The strike also wasn't about who runs the mining industry or how best to run the industry for the benefit of miners and the nation as a whole – it was about a last-ditch stand against the decimation of the industry to a dozen super pits - then to privatise them along with the frenzied privatisation of other nationalised industries unleashed by the Conservative Government in the 1990s.

In 1926, A J Cook in his pamphlet called The Nine Days wrote: *"The British coal owners have declared publicly... that they would never again meet the miners representatives, never again submit to national agreements and that they would insist on district settlements – thus break up the power, the unity and solidarity of the mineworker – which had developed markedly since the building of the Miners Federation".*

It happened to another generation of mining workers whose forefathers had campaigned for nationalisation. This time the coal owners (the state as represented by the Conservative Government 1979 to 1997) carried through their threats.

The postal workers face similar dilemmas at the time that this account is published. If the Government can break up the Royal Mail postal service into competing sections or sub-sections, such as sorting, letters and parcels delivery, regional and local delivery services and so on, then they hope to emasculate the strength of the postal workers union, the CWU, in the process. It is unfinished business for the Tories as well as New Labour. The battle to save the Royal Mail has commenced. Its similarities with the demise of the coal industry need not be repeated.

Royal Mail's chief executive Adam Crozier (former FA chief executive) and newly appointed chairman of the board, Donald Brydon, seek to break up the organisations they work in and deal with people on a local level to suit their corporate strategies of divide and rule. Shareholding and investment clubs take precedence over the needs of the workforce and the industry itself.

To argue that the industry needs private investment to become more efficient and profitable is nonsense. The industry is profitable as an operation. Trade unions offer modern and innovative ideas for change every day and are ignored.

The CWU deserves enormous credit for the restraint they have shown over the attempts to break up our national postal service. The New Labour Government offers no respite to the attacks on the terms and conditions of Britain's postal workers.

The lessons learned during the miners' struggles can be heeded by all workers engaged in large industries facing breaking up and privatisation. Arthur Horner's maxim that labour is no more than a commodity to the employers, where the trade union has to place itself in a position so that employers buy their labour based on the collective terms and conditions and standards of the existing workforce, is still worth heeding. All new employees of the postal service are now part-time and non-pensionable. A significant struggle to retain fair pay and conditions is inevitable.

Railworkers face similar issues after their industry has been broken up into dozens of contractor and outsourcing companies supplying the rail industry. To retain a fighting trade union based on the historical principles of maintaining the living standards and rights of its members requires perseverance, tenacity and embracing socialist and trade union principles fought for over the past two centuries.

The lessons of the strike

So, 25 years on, the battles that we faced as miners before, during and after the strike are still continuing for working people. There has, inevitably, been much written about the lessons of the strike and much of it has been written in a way that misleads about the significance and real lessons of that period.

Today, there is a new generation of young trade union organisers who know that the "official" accounts of the strike are distorted and seek to find out the real lessons of the strike. When asked about this, I know there are many lessons to be taken on board and I hope my account has helped add knowledge for that new generation of trade unionists and socialists.

But nowadays, there seems to be a desire in the media to present things in the form of lists. So, if pressed to draw out some lessons that I think need to be absorbed and passed on then I would list the following:

● The need for a democratic fighting trade union with a strong Leadership within one recognisable legal structure. The NUM was a number of separately registered unions deferring certain functions to the national union but not all. Including the right to call area ballots of the members. This was the mechanism used to introduce the incentive schemes in the late 1970s. Newly merged unions should heed this lesson.

- On-going availability of education: training and learning in trade union studies in economic and political awareness by the workforce.
- Regular elections of all full-time officials as well as lay officials.
- Know your industry well – understand how it works and its complexities - study how it works and its position in the local and global markets.
- Become a shadow of the management structure but maintain your independence fighting for your rights.
- Equal representation on the governing bodies of industry with right of recall of officials.
- Be prepared to fight for what you believe to be right for your industry and for your fellow workers.
- The realisation that a desirable form of human, political and economic society based on fair and equitable distribution of wealth and power will not come about by a passive trade union and Labour movement is paramount.

Ian Isaac, *December 2009*

Appendices

Bibliography

Books

- The Man from the Alamo, John Humphries, 2004,
  Wales Books, Glyndwr Publishing
- Scargill and the Miners, Michael Crick, 1985, Penguin Books
- The Merthyr Rising, Gwyn A. Williams, 1978, Biddles Ltd, Guildford, Surrey
- Revolt on the Clyde, William Gallacher, 1990, Lawrence & Wishart, London
- We struggled to laugh Barnsley Miners Wives Action Group,
  1987, Published with support from Sheffield City Council
  and assistance of Heeley Writers' Group
- Coal Miners Union, Mikhail Srebny, 1986, Profizdat
- The miners' fight for jobs - Our day will come, Mike Freeman,
  1985, Junius Publications
- Justice - The Miners' Strike 1984-85, Campaign Group of Labour MPs,
  1986, Verso
- The Myth of Worker's Control, Arthur Scargill and Peggy Kahn,
  1980, University of Leeds and University of Nottingham
- Birmingham and the Miners Strike, Paul Mackey, 1987, Birmingham TUC
- On War, Carl Von Clauswiz,
  Uncompleted Works 1981, Wordsworth Classics, 1997
- The Nine Days, The story of the General Strike told by the Miners;
  Secretary A.J. Cook, Reprinted 1971,Cymric Federation Press, Cardiff
- The Story of the Miners Strike, Labour Research, April 1972
- Striking Back, Welsh Campaign for civil and political liberties and NUM, June 2005
- A Civil War without Guns - 20 years on, Ken Smith,
  May 2004, Socialist Productions
- Inside Cowley, Alan Thornett, 1993, Porcupine Books

Reports

- Annual Report 1984, National Union of Mineworkers, 1984
- Report of Special Delegate Conference November 1984,
  National Union of Mineworkers, 1984
- Decisions of the Annual Conference 1986,
  National Union of Mineworkers, 1986
- Minutes of Special Area Executive Council Meeting,
  National Union of Mineworkers, 1984
- Annual Conference Agenda and Annual Report for 1984-1986,
  George Rees, May 1986

Pamphlets

- We must fight to secure the present strength and future growth of the coal industry,
  Sir Derek Ezra, 1978, National Coal Board
- What is the future?, Iron and Steel Traders Confederation,
  National Union of Railwaymen and National Union of Mineworkers, 1981
- The future of Socialism, Neil Kinnock,
  1986, Fabian Society
- A Charter for Young Workers, Labour Party Young Socialists,
  1974, Labour Party
- Anti Nuclear Campaign - The Costs of Nuclear Power, Colin Sweet
- Miners in the Eighties, Arthur Scargill, Yorkshire NUM
- The Miners and the Battle for Britain, The National Executive Committee,
  National Union of Mineworkers, National Union of Mineworkers
- "New Realism" The politics of fear, Arthur Scargill,
  1987, Merthyr Tydfil Trades Union Council
- Economic aspects of the Coal Industry dispute, Andrew Glyn, 1984

Printed here are various documents relating to the period covered by When We Were Miners. They are reprinted as they were in the original - rather than being edited - to give the reader a feel for the issues of the time.

Extracts from St Johns NUM Minute Book 1984/85

Keeping the Pit open by going through the Modified review Procedure:

Minutes 15th September 1985

The Vice chairman and secretary reported on the National review meeting held 11th September at Hobart House London and commented on the excellent presentation of the case to keep the Pit open.
The NCB had agreed that they would listen to the case and report back to a full NCB Board meeting on 4th Oct 1985. Therefore the status quo would prevail until full knowledge of the modified procedure was to hand.

In discussion and following a question on buy back of National insurance stamps it was agreed to draw up a Newssheet to explain the qualifying entitlements to dole in 1986 should redundancies occur before and after December 31st 1985.

It was agreed not to give financial assistance to men who attended the Lobby of the review meeting as it was made clear that the Lobby was voluntary.

Lodge Committee 27th September 2009.

The campaign to keep the Pit open continued...
UWIST Labour Club. John Potts Committeeman reported on a good day at the Freshers fair. 6 Copies of the Independent enquiry report to keep the Pit Open were sold.

Special Committee meeting 8th October 1985.

The Secretary informed the committee that rumours concerning the NCB's new Tactic of insisting on 12 weeks notice of redundancy where appropriate which meant that future benefits would be affected if notice begins after the 9th October. A full explanation of the situation wsa given. After a lengthy discussion it was agreed that the following resolution be put before a mass general meeting the following day: " Do you agree to continue to to appeal through the Colliery Review procedure against the NCB Area decision to recommend closure; bearing in mind that the NCB intend to apply the 12 weeks notice to men applying for redundancy. The Lodge recommends that you vote in favour. This was carried unanimously.

Following day...
General meeting of St Johns NUM Lodge membership.9th October 1985

The secretary gave a full updated report on the situation . After a discussion was held on a question and answer session on redundancies a vote was taken and recorded as 165 in Favour and 106 votes against. It was declared by the Chairman that we carry on the fight to keep the Pit open through the appeal procedure.

Special Lodge Committee meeting 11th October 1985.

National Demonstration against Pit Closures Barnsley October 19th It was agreed to support a delegation to attend where the National president was speaking provided that it was within the financial capability of the Lodge. It was left to the Secretary to help make arrangements financially. A notice is to be placed at the pit for Volunteers.

The Secretary read out a Geological survey commissioned with Malcolm Blanchford which showed that the NCB claims of an 18meter fault in the 6ft was certainly spurious and false.

Complaints were made about lack of maintenance in the B1 face.

Lodge Committee 27th October 1985

The Chairman read out a letter from Ian Isaac, Lodge Secretary enquiring of the support of the Lodge to stand for the Position of President   in the Area.
 A letter was also readout from Mr Terry Thomas Miners Agent making a similar request. The Secretary explained his reasons for standing which involved putting forward the claim that he would campaign for a Miners President on a miners wage which was Lodge policy and that the experience of the Pits closing in the past 3 months demonstrated that much needed to be done with the :Leadership of the Area. Mr Phillip White indicated that he would do all he could to assist in whichever way he could to organise the campaign.
It was proposed by Phillip White and seconded by Mr John Potts that this Lodge nominate Ian Isaac Lodge Secretary for the Post of President in South Wales.

Following meetings recently with Bold NUM Officials from Lancashire it was agreed to attend a joint committee to be held in Birmingham of Collieries under threat.

The Secretary reported on the situation in the S12 face which has resulted in the Manager getting away with scuttling the face. In the meantime the feelings in the Pit were mixed as to what course of action to take. It was felt overall that we still had a responsibility to the decisions of the general meetings of the general body of membership which in simple terms meant that we continue to fight through the review procedure and if the Pit is shut then let the NCB shit it – not the Lodge or the men.

It was agreed that the Secretary write an appropriate letter to the Glamorgan Gazette taking up the issue that the Lodge had not said that it was redundancy benefits that were to be thrown away in defending the Pit. This difficult question needs proper explanation

Committee meeting 10th November 1985.

Lodge nomination of Mr Ian Isaac for Area President. It was unanimously agreed to sponsor Mr Isaac in a vigorous campaign to include leaflets, posters and members of the lodge committee and rank and file members to be involved in distribution of same around the Coalfield.
Mr Phillip White outlined the extent to which the campaign need to develop.

Ballot for President. It was noted that 323 Ballot papers would be given to the Lodge.

Copy letters of the NCBs intentions following their October 4th Board meeting was read out. This vindicated the stand of the Lodge in that the NCB Area Director was not able to make known his closure arrangements, the Lodge having boycotted the area meeting.

Maesteg Community Council request for a donation towards street lighting this year. It was decided not to make a donation towards the £3.385 cost and the Lodge would suggest that perhaps Mr Islwyn Edwards would himself make good any short fall as the Chairman of the Chamber of Trade who is of the view that the "Closure of St Johns Colliery would have little if any impact on the economic well being of the town of Maesteg."

Chairman reported on Rumours concerning men transferring to Tower colliery. In view of the fact that this had occurred without consultation the Lodge Officers would intervene to ensure proper consultation.

The Chairmen then gave his considered opinions on the situation facing the membership at the Pit. He gave three options: 1. To keep the pit open. 2. Let the NCB do their dirty work and close the Pit. 3 Force the NCB through the review procedure. During discussion other opinions were expressed including: Get as much mileage out fo the Pit as possible, The Lodge to calla general meeting in view of petition going around the pit. That we consider a press release that we declare that we are unable to pursue the fight further and blame the NCB for scuttling the Mine through their actions.
In the end it was decided to await the outcome of a meeting this evening in Garw Colliery over their future and await developments to see if we can have a joint campaign. To monitor the situation day by day and call a Lodge Committee meeting if an event of fundamental proportions threatens.

The Secretary reported on the under manning of the Bute face and it was agreed to meet the new under manger about this.

12 days later

Special Lodge Committee meeting 22nd November 1985

Ron Roberts presided. Charles White Chairman was in attendance after falling ill over the previous weekend. He asked that Mr Roberts chair the meeting and the subsequent General meeting.

The Secretary reported on the satiations in the Pit. The internal memorandum from Mr C.J.Davies Area Director (Phillip Weeks having retired) had a significant effect on the attitudes in the Mine which was compounded with the debilitating affect on moral of the closure of the S12 Face which left men loyal to the lodge feeling that it was inevitable that the Pit would close in the near future. In view of the deadline that the Area Director had imposed for the 22nd November 85 for the processing (before Christmas) of redundancies or Transfer with the additional offer of £800 offered by Christmas for transfers. This had and was still having an effect on attitudes in the mine. The Secretary then read out a letter from the Colliery Manager where he remained vague in response to the Lodge request for information on the manning requirements in the Bute district now that the salvage programme was complete in the S District. This at least gave the Lodge some latitude on the question of a slimed down workforce being able to run the mine.

A number of points were raised in discussion including a 47 named petition which it was decided not to affect our thinking being totally insufficient as a body of opinion. What mattered was the dignity and situation of the men and the Lodge.

It was eventually agreed to put the following recommendation to the Lodge.

"That this general meeting of St John Lodge NUM charges its Officers and Committee to negotiate with the local management and the NCB the following demands:

1) That all men in the NUM at the Mine who wish to avail themselves of of redundancy in time to sogn the Dole before the 2nd January 10986 and be off books by the latest 21st December 1985 be allowed to do so.
2) That all men in the NUM at the Mine who wish to immediately transfer to other collieries by the 14th December be allowed to do so.
3) That all men in the NUM at the mine who wish to remain on the books of St Johns Colliery and remain whilst the case of St Johns Colliery is heard in the new Modified procedure be allowed to do so.

In doing so this general meeting condemns the blackmailing tactics of the NCB in creating an hostile atmosphere in the mine. It also condemns the NCB for stragling the Pit of routine investment and have been ruthless in their breach of assurances given to the Mining Unions that " Nothing would be done to prejudiced the outcome of the appeal against closure."

A further general meeting will be held on Thursday 26th November to report back on progress and receive a national report on developments in the St John's Appeal. Bearing in mind that the Lodge Committee will remain committed, ensuring that no decisions will be taken by the general meeting that will prevent men avoiding loss of benefits both DHSS (Department of Health and Social Security) and RMPS (Redundant Miners Payment Scheme) in 1986.

"Concern was express that due to pressures of protocol that Mr Arthur Scargill was unable to address the meeting and that Area Officials had read into the request that the Maesteg Communities Action Committee plans for a Public meeting in support of the campaign to keep mining in Maesteg was linked to the Area Presidential campaign. This was not the case and it was deplorable that the Area Officials had used it to prevent Mr Scargill speaking, and it spun off into the Lodge request for Mr Scargill to address the General Meeting."

The Area officials had intervened to prevent a genuine request by a Lodge facing closure of their mine forever in order to protect their reputations and protocols as area officials. It is worth noting that not one volunteered to attend the General meeting of St Johns Lodge.

General meeting of St John Lodge NUM 22nd November 1985

"In the General meeting that followed the Lodge Recommendation failed to carry by 106 votes in Favour and 185 votes against.

In view of the rejection of the Lodge recommendation it was declared that the Lodge Officers would now approach the Colliery Manager the following day to inform him that we can no longer advise our members to continue production at St John's Colliery and that we are now prepared to negotiate transfers and redundancies in line with the NCB memorandum signed by CJ Davies. R Gwynne, R Boswell, A Collins, C Jury acted as tellers in the meeting."

Signed R Robert Acting Chairman

Special Committee Meeting 8th December 1985

The Chairman explained that the meeting had been called to deal with a letter received from the General Secretary George Rees and to discuss financial issues confronting the Lodge and also to discuss financial matters outstanding in relation to the tragic Death of the Lodge Chairman Mr. Charles White.

The letter from the General Secretary was also signed by the Area President and although dated 22nd November didn't arrive until the 28th November, the day before the ballot for area President.

Concern was expressed by a number of committeemen that this was in fact blatant interference in the election by the Area Official themselves and the Area Executive. The Lodge disassociated itself with the article that appeared in the Western mail on the 18th November and also previous articles which the area officials and executive didn't make a song and dance about as they are on this occasion. It was proposed and seconded that the secretary write back to the General Secretary explaining that in our considered opinion we have broken no rules and that we consider that the Area Officials had interfered in the conduct of the Ballot with Circular Ref No85/155.

Area consultative election. A Letter was read out from Cwm Lodge requesting our support for in the forthcoming ballot for a vacant position on the Area consultative committee for their Secretary Billy Lidden. It was agreed unanimously to vote for Billy Lidden.

In returning to the question of the Ballot for president the compensation Secretary Mr Phillip White expressed concern about a letter sent to Mr Ian Isaac in person on the 19th November 1985. which was contrary to understandings that he and the Secretary had with the General Secretary over the contents of the election leaflets and posters. An understanding had been reached that the slogan on the front of the main leaflet would be deleted ie " A miners President on a miners wage". Where this phrase appeared elsewhere in the leaflets it was recognized as being okay in that it was qualified by explanation in the section dealing with 'Union Democracy' and also at the back page of the election leaflet.. At the EC meeting and over the Telephone with Mr White that this was okay so the Lodge were surprised to have received a letter saying to the contrary and that the words be deleted on all literature. Again we deny breaking any rules. It was agreed to reply accordingly to explain the truth of the matter and that if the Area officials wanted to come and meet the Lodge that was Okay.

It was agreed to write to the General Secretary requesting the funds that the Lodge had in its possession for other purposes during the strike to be returned. This was estimated at £25,000. The Lodge would also request its money for year end commitments so that £10,000 would be a help.

It was agreed that committee attendance fees be paid before Christmas as we had done in the past.

It was agreed to donate £10 to Garth Senior citizens and £50 to Maesteg Boxing club. It was agreed to reimburse expenses to Thomas Fullen, from Ireland who had attended the funeral of Charles White. This was in view of the fact that he was unemployed and had been a great support raising funds during the strike. He paid his last savings to attend the funeral.
Financial matters in relation to Charles White, Chairman of St John's Lodge NUM now Deceased.

It was agreed to pay cropped 8 shifts deducted when Mr White came into conflict with the management over Trade Union time off to attend to Lodge duties. This to be paid to his widow Mrs Jean White. Also accumulated committee attendance fees and a donation of £250 towards a headstone or for such other expense resulting from his death that the family sees fit to spend.

It was also agreed to pay for a photo of the Lodge committee and include a portrait of Mr White the former chairman as well.

It was agreed to commission Gary Bevan and Hazel Gittings of the Tondu Photo workshop.

Special Committee meeting 14th December 1985

Ron Roberts presided.
The Chairman explained that the Secretary had received a letter from the General Secretary in relation to the ballot held for S Wales Area president.

The Secretary then read out the letter which stated that the Lodge should attend a meeting of the executive council on the 7th January 1986 and went on to say that two Lodges had made allegations of misdemeanors by "your members at their respective Pits. It went to say that there were allegations in relation to interference by militant organisation in the ballot. Also that leaflets were distributed after instructions had been given that certain words should be taken out.

After a lengthy discussion it was agreed to write a letter along with others denying any misdemeanors by our members. To our knowledge no rules or etiquettes had been infringed.

Surprise was expressed in the committee that what ever the allegations were they were (against the St Johns lodge members) not put in writing. If any Lodge had a complaint against another lodge they should put these in writing. The General Secretary should at least give a summary of facts.

The Executive appear to be exceeding their powers in this matter. It was agreed to enquire as the details of the so called allegations.. If complaints were made against the distribution of literature at the Pits then they too should be put in writing to us. It was further agreed that the Lodge would have to consider any written complaints before agreeing to appear before the executive council or any body set up by the executive council.

The compensation secretary then gave a report on the campaign and the involvement of rank and file miners (20 rank and file members and 12 committeemen volunteered to distribute literature in support of the campaign. In all a team of 35) commenting that their conduct was exemplary throughout the presidential campaign. The committee endorsed the expenditure of the Lodge on the campaign and took into account an outstanding bill (for Gibbs Printers) for the cost of literature for the campaign.

Signed R Roberts

Committee meeting 5th January 1986

A discussion ensued as to the intentions of the Area full time Officials and EC with regard to the ill-founded rumours and accusations of breaking rules

And etiquette during the Presidential campaign. The Secretary read out the correspondence he had sent and the letter agin to appear before the EC on the 7th January. After a full ranging discussion it was decided that the Lodge would not attend the EC due to their vague references to misdemeanors etc. IT was agreed to reiterate our disbelief as to this campaign of smear mongering embarked upon by the EC. The Secretary would write back explaining that if the contents of the allegations were given to the lodge then the Lodge would attend at the EC. As it is the Lodge Officers would be in dark as to any questioning on supposed misdemeanors.

Letters were read out from the General Secretary on the Financial position of the lodge. A request was turned down for an advance of the Lodges own funds we used during the strike when the area NUM funds were sequestrated....

Result of the Area Election for President. The circular was read out. It agreed to note the good showing of the Lodge Secretary despite the interference of the area Officials with a circular to lodges the day before the ballot. It was agreed that the Lodge complain about the interference in the Ballot by the Area Officials.

A discussion ensued over the treatment given to the Lodge Secretary by the management and the NCB. Whilst other men were allowed to transfer to the Pit of their choice the secretary was informed that he had no option but to accept a job in the Avon Methane plant or leave the industry.

It was obvious that collusion had taken place between Colliery managers to prevent Mr Isaac having a job in a Colliery which was his desire. It was agreed to write to the Miners Agent complaining about this victimization..

The Committee went over the 1984 financial books and agreed the contents of the Financial report.

Committee meeting 19th January 1986

Lodge Finances. It was agreed in view of the difficulties involved to supply details of current debts to the Area of all outstanding bills including the payment of Lodge Honorariums, benevolent fund and loss of earnings for officers of the Lodge during the presidential campaign etc. The question of the monies belong to the Benevolent fund used for Picketing be taken up at a later date when the Areas finances are settled and after the view of retired members have been sought.

The Secretary reported that although he had not been informed in writing he was informed by the Miners Agent that the Lodge was wound up. The Secretary informed the meeting that he would not accept any limited membership dues for 1986 and asked that the limited members be advised as to any new arrangements for collection and the information on the new Housecoal scheme , pensions etc.

Mrs E Harris husband died. Agreed to provide assistance for pension etc.
Wil John. Wife died. Agreed a grant of £20 be awarded.

The committee noted that Vi John who had been of great assistance to the Lodge during the Miners Strike was the subject of hostile abuse by the Labour Party Secretary. The Lodge would make its concerns known over this matter.

Special Lodge Committee meeting held 19th March 1984

[This meeting decisions regarding use of Lodges own funds was to set the seeds of a subsequent dispute between the Lodge and the Area Officials of the NUM which tarnished their reputation for all time in the minds of the St Johns NUM Members and Lodge Officers.

Charles White Presided.
"...The chairman explained that this was a special meeting of the Lodge and apologized for short notice and that there being other room available bar the Lodge Secretary's Office for the meeting.
Both he and Secretary had been to Pontypridd this day and it was necessary to make certain decisions in relation to Lodge Funds and finances for Picketing.

The Secretary then gave a report on the situation. That we were to sent 6 months advance contributions as the Area feared that the Unions funds could be in danger of being sequestrated. They had seen David Kennedy, Area Finance Officer who advised that all funds that the Lodge had be taken out of all accounts with the bank etc and the money placed in Safe deposit boxes or such like and utilised for Picketing and traveling expenses. That we should keep a record of what was spent as the Area (NUM) will reimburse when the strike is over as on previous occasions. The reason for this was the NGA (Union) had recently been sequestrated and even a local branch unemployed funds frozen which placed in the firing line even our welfare and benevolent funds.

After discussion it was agreed that the 4 officers undertook the safe keeping of the cash and utilize as necessary for picketing. It was agreed that Ron Roberts would now act as Treasurer and J(Jimmy) Jones would assist with Picketing allocations and paying out the men..
It was further agreed that Colin Day be responsible for Safety at the Mine.
Due to the fact that we need to act as a joint Lodges it was agreed to fall in line with this and meet when issues arises."

Committee meeting 9th February 1986

Phil White deputised for Ron Roberts

The Secreary reported that he and Ron Roberts had met the General Secretary, together with Des Dutfield, President Elect and Mr. David Kennedy Finance Officer. The outstanding debts had been met by the area officials and it was noted that nearly £2,000 was owed to the lodge for members contributions making the outstanding debts including £1,700 overdraft to be £3,400. A letter was read out from the General Secretary which quoted rule 50 of the S. Wales Rule book and stated that this was a final payment to St Johns Lodge.

The Lodge then suspended its business to receive a delegation from Mr. Thos. Kearle former chairman, Ivor Colliery former committeeman and John Jones Retired member. The delegation wanted to know the exact position regarding the benevolent fund money that was loaned to the Area for picketing in 1984. The Secretary then gave a full account to the delegation of the fate of this money and that there was extreme reluctance by the Area Officials and executive to pay back this money. The delegation pointed out that this money had been raised to provide for benevolent issues as agreed by the Lodge. That it was the responsibility of the Lodge to respect the wishes of former workmen and call a general meeting to decided the fate of the money once it is paid back.

The feeling was so strong that Mr. Kearle said that they should meet with George Rees Genarl Secretary straight away to demand the money back.. The whole of the Lodge committee recall how the area Officials calling for Lodges to spend their own funds drawn locally. Mr. Kearle and his delegation were thanked for their views and contribution to the meeting and the delegation then left the meeting.

The Committee agreed to apply to the General Secretary for the outstanding amount of £21,000 approx. under the responsibilities of the area under rule 50.

It was noted that the Secretary had now been informed that we were still in being as Lodge by the Miners Agent in a meeting to form a Lodge out of the Maesteg Washeries. Tondu and Ogmore Washery. The Miners agent having ruled out of order and against the constitution a motion nominating Ian Isaac as Compensation Secretary of the new Lodge because, as he put it, St Johns Lodge was still in being as a Lodge and Ian Isaac was still its secretary.

Terry Thomas as Miners Agent had his own back for me standing against him in the Presidents ballot which he and I both failed to be elected in.

11 days later.
Committee meeting 23rd February 1986.

It was agreed to write to the Miners agent complaining against the insensitive and cynical manner in which the Lodge was wound up and seeking clarification on the situation.

No reply had been received regarding reimbursement of the Lodge's funds from the Area.

The Joint Lodges banner. It was agreed that a suitable fixing be arranged for display of the Banner in the Nantyffyllon Institute.

It was agreed to have a final group photograph.

It was agreed to meet again to go over the 1985 finance report.

20th April 1986
Meeting of members of the former Lodge Committee with responsibilities for the Benevolent Fund.

Also in attendance were Mr. Thos. Kearle, Ivor Colliery and John Jones. Formers members of St Johns Lodge Committee.

The Secretary reported that he had received a letter from the General Secretary in reply to our detailed request to reimburse £20,971.70p to the Benevolent fund. The letter stated briefly that "after along discussion the executive council decided that they cannot accede to your request to reimburse the St Johns Benevolent fund £20,971.70p." The Secretary stated that that he felt stunned by the whole experience and could think of no logical reason for such a decision. He was present at the relevant EC meeting and lost the vote and was in a minority of one. He believed there was an element of vindictiveness in the decision. He went on to explain that the problem was compounded by the fact that ¾ of million of S.Wales funds were still sequestrated by the Courts and the National Imprest account was tied up as well. The Secretary stated he was at a loss as to what advice to give except to lodge an immeadite appeal due to this fact. He felt that perhaps we should approach things in a different way until the financial situation became more clear in a few months time.

A wide ranging discussion then ensued with respect to men who were retired and over the age of 50 stating that we will take action against this decision with the feelings of the members we need to take things up individually rather than lose this money. The secretary stated that at the end of the day he would consider taking legal action to get the money back but only as a last resort.

It was suggested that we raise with other Lodges that Pontypridd (S Wales NUM) had gone back on its word . This money was used in an emergency to help the decisions of the Area Executive who called us out on strike.

We should quote the rule book back at them. Especially the statement" Area to be responsible for the Financial Liabilities of Lodges when Pits Close".

In view of the fact that the EC has taken over our responsibilities and liabilities that they should contribute and provide for a function for all St Johns men on closure.. In view of the fact that other closed lodges have had one with presentations of lamps, ties and badges we should ask for the same treatment. Phil White proposed that the Secretary raise this with the General Secretary.

Mr Thomas Kearle enquired if we had any objections to the retired Officials going to George Rees (General Secretary S.Wales NUM). It was felt that this may help put pressure to bear on the Area Officials concerning the claim that the men were demanding their money back and a retirement function with dignity.

Meeting of former Lodge Committee 8th June 1986.

Ron Roberts presided.
Mr Ian Isaac reported that he had met with the Area General Secretary who now appeared to accept that something could be done about the retirement functions. He had informed the General Secretary that the estimated cost of a retirement function was in the region of £10,000. Also that a small firm had been set up under NCB enterprises to make hand made Figurines of a miner on wooden plinths and would be appropriate for the large numbers of men under 50. It was agreed that Mr Isaac go ahead to organise the presentation figurines and for the full account of cost to be sent to the General Secretary. Based on the report today and cost of the retirement functions this would cost £12,000 for functions, a trust fund and donations to Nanty Library.

It was agreed to call a further meeting when there was further developments to report.

In the event a function evening and Presentation was held for all men who were over the age of 50 when the Colliery closed in December 1985. This reduced the monies owed to the fund to £11,854.70p

The former lodge continued to make presentation to the Area Officials of the NUM to help pay for a function and a presentation for men under the age of 50 at the time of the closure of St John's colliery.

We were told that men transferring to other collieries would fall under the auspices of their new lodges in terms of benevolent considerations.

Meeting held 29th November 1986

A Decision was taken in a meeting of former NUM lodge members. For the purpose of decision making and dissolution of the fund only those members of the NUM contributing to the fund as at the 22nd December 1985 will be able to make proposals and vote. All other Beneficiaries of the fund as it would be in normal conditions are entitled to ask questions and make statements.

It was resolved that the Officers and committee of the fund continue to pursue their legal responsibilities in respect of outstanding monies owed to the fund and continue to press for a retirement function and or presentation for men under the age of 50. That a further meeting be held in January 1987 to review circumstances. In the meantime the meeting resolved not to dissolve the St John's Benevolent Fund.

The fund was never dissolved and is not to this day.

1986 Welcome Address

Idwal Isaac

Chairman, Maesteg Town Council on the occasion that Arthur Scargill addressed a public meeting in the Maesteg Town Hall as Part of the re-elect Arthur Scargill campaign. There was one disinter in the hall that night Jack Williams whose attempt to heckle was drowned out from the back of a packed hall with over 600 in attendance. He left the meeting realising he was in a minority of one that evening such was the strength of support for Arthur and the Miners in the Hall.

Chairman, Ladies and Gentlemen. On behalf of Maesteg Community Council, may I extend a warm welcome to Arthur Scargill, Laurie Prescott, and James Motlasi President of the South African Mineworkers.

Perhaps I should express astonishment not to see Arthur carrying a giant fork and sprouting horns from his head; because, if we are to believe the media, he is the Devil Incarnate. Such is the power of the enemies propaganda. In fact, he is a courageous man prepared to be vilified for his principles and beliefs.

I don't want to comment on the conflict between the NUM and British .Coal. on the new Disciplinary Code – I'll leave that to Arthur's expertise. However, I will make some observations on the present Government, and the Labour Movement's reaction to it.

It appears strange, perhaps a paradox of our time, that when we are experiencing the most reactionary Government since the adult franchise of 1929, that all opposition parties are preaching the gospel of moderation. It is a Government which governs by secrecy and outright political expediency. It has emasculated the NHS and other social services, it is gradually destroying the democracy of local government; and it is now intent on finalizing the decimation of the Welsh mining valleys. It is a Government that has uprooted, and continue to uproot, the rights and freedoms gained by working people since 1945. Yet we are being advised by many leaders in the Labour Movement to exercise moderation and realism in the way we react to a gang of ruthless bandits raiding the granary of our dignities and rights to a future free from social deprivation. A Government that has contemptuously pushed aside moderation in its attacks upon working people, while it pillage and rapes state assets in an orgy of profiteering that makes 19th century laissez-faire look like a Vicar's Church Hall Bingo session.

As well as being urged to be moderate, we are asked to believe that the working class, like the Dodo bird, is now extinct. Somehow or other, working people, who comprise 70% of the population, and whose only source of income is wages or social benefits, and who still remain on the low, or lowest income groups, have now become classless. What a ridiculous idea.

Certainly, relative to the pre-war era, living standards among working people have greatly increased with access to home ownership, colour T.V. and Videos, and foreign holidays. Yet again, relative to the wealth they create, they still remain on the bottom of the pyramid of economic wealth. Annual increases in wages and benefits will not cover the erosion of social services in health, education, transport, and other social services that is now taking place. Items that constitute the social wage, which is so essential to the economic security of this supposedly extinct class. That is why the access to Tory affluence is illusionary. The continuing privatisation of state assets is designed to destroy the social wage, to turn the clock back to longer hours and lower wages, and a Victorian, workhouse-based charity.

Indiscipline private enterprise, with a laissez-faire approach, ruined the essential industries in this country before and at the beginning of the 20th century – that is why governments, all Western governments, had to apply state discipline. The consequences, the full brunt of the rapacious and irresponsible private enterprise, given free reign, fell upon the working people. History is beginning to repeat itself – yet we are being advised to be moderate.

At the last Liberal Conference (Harrogate) a delegate said: "We are the enemy of Thatcherism and the enemy of Socialism." He should have completed his slogan by adding: "But a friend of Capitalism."

The signals of moderation and realism are designed to assure capitalism that the political opposition parties do not pose a threat to it. I am sure that there won't be any reassuring signals from the speakers on the platform here tonight.

A Job without a Pit

The Militant, 1986.

14 MILITANT 14 February 1986

Miners

Coal Board attempt to isolate activist

THE CLOSURE of St Johns colliery in South Wales just before Christmas marked the end of one of the most determined campaigns against pit closures seen in the British coalfield. The experience of that nine month campaign has now been transferred, along with the St Johns men, to the few remaining pits in South Wales.

The warm reception they have received is an indication of the authority the men have built up during the strike and in their fight to keep their pit open.

The recent presidential election saw ex-St Johns Lodge secretary, Ian Isaac, win around 23 per cent of the vote against the sitting vice-president and ex-vice president.

High price

This also reflects the growing support for the initiative, combativity and strength of the St Johns Lodge Committee.

However, the price of standing firm for the interests of their members has meant victimisation by the NCB of some of the best NUM activists.

The National Coal Board in South Wales have embarked on a campaign of blatant victimisation against ex-Lodge Secretary and South Wales NUM Executive member, Ian Isaac, in a deliberate attempt to drive him out of the industry.

One and a half weeks before Christmas Isaac approached the pit manager with a request for himself and five other miners to transfer to Blaenant colliery. This procedure was in line with an agreement reached with management on 23 November which provided for men to be transferred to the colliery of their choice.

Nevertheless, the transfer request was rejected on the grounds that a job had already been allocated for him elsewhere. This makes him the only miner in St Johns to be allocated a job by management.

The job on offer was in the methane plant at Blaengwynfi 30 miles from the nearest pit with only three men being employed there. One on mornings, one on afternoons and one on nights.

The prospect of Isaac working alone day after day, prompted the manager to remark: "I can see you leaving the industry". To which he replied: "No chance—I want the same as everyone else and to be allowed the preference of a pit. The only way I'll leave the industry is if I'm sacked".

Manoeuvres

The manager again rejected his request despite the fact that three local miners from the village wanted to work in the methane plant, which is on their doorstep.

The manager made doubly sure Isaac would not work in Blaenant by informing the other five miners that all transfers to Blaenant had been stopped, which resulted in another two men being forced to take redundancy.

After this abortive interview Isaac contacted the manager of Betwys colliery, West Wales, who was desperately seeking underground workers to replace the over 50s in the pit. Despite Isaac's known trade union activity the manager agreed to sign him on, along with four other St Johns men, the following day.

Two hours after saying Isaac could start, the Betwys manager phoned back to say that there was no longer an opening for him, but the other four could start as agreed.

The NCB are determined to keep Ian Isaac isolated from the mainstream of members. The NUM in South Wales must now fight tooth and nail against the victimisation of one of its leaders.

The St Johns Committee have registered an official complaint through the conciliation procedure demanding he be allowed the same rights as other miners. Rank and file miners should protest vigorously against the Board's action and give full support to the union's efforts to allow him to work in a pit of his choice.

By a Militant reporter

NUM (South Wales Area)
BALLOT FOR AREA PRESIDENT

VOTE FOR

IAN ISAAC

A MINERS' PRESIDENT
ON A MINER'S WAGE

Ian Isaac's original election leaflet.

Hem Heath bonus victory

MINERS AT Hem Heath in North Staffs have forced a humiliating climbdown by the NCB management over bonus payments.

Management tried their usual tactic of attempting to divide the men by altering the normal system of bonus payment.

Over 250 attended a meeting, despite threats by the pit manager that anyone attending the gathering would lose their Sunday work. Twelve members of the UDM voted with the rest to hold a demo on Monday 3 February.

Despite the ravings of NCB management, miners at Hem Heath have proved more than once since the end of the strike, that they are still prepared to carry on the fight.

Events such as this will also prove to the majority of the UDM members that only the NUM can organise the continuing struggle against the NCB.

By Andy Bentley

Kinsley Drift adopts fighting tactics

Memories of a Titanic Struggle

Glamorgan Gazette, November 11, 1999, Millenium Memories.

MINERS' LEADER: Former St John's lodge secretary Ian Isaac pictured on the site of the old NCB training centre at Tondu where he started his mining career 30 years ago.

Memories of a titanic struggle

WHEN the news came through that St John's Colliery, Maesteg was to be shut the miners waged a titanic struggle to save it.

The man who led them through these tumultuous times – and who played a leading part in the year-long miners' strike – was lodge secretary Ian Isaac.

Ian, who left mining in 1989 and now works as a development officer with a charity for the mentally ill, has vivid memories of the strike and the fight to save mining in Maesteg.

He served on the national executive of the South Wales NUM throughout these years.

"We had gone back to work in March 1985 at the end of the strike as a strong and united lodge to a pit which was in tip top shape," he said.

But within weeks, the NCB announced that they were putting St John's through the newly set-up review procedure with a view to closure.

And the fight was on.

"We knew that the pit had economic reserves and that it could be operated at a profit," he said.

They launched a campaign under the banner of "Keep Mining in Maesteg" and set up a special action group with members of the miners' support group which mobilised the community.

"We had terrific support from the people of the valley both during the strike and after," he said.

The men engaged a former NCB mining engineer to provide them with geological evidence and also brought in Oxford economist Andrew Glyn to look at the arguments.

"Every argument the NCB brought forward for closure we were able to counter," he said.

"We agreed to slim down the workforce from 780 to 450 and all men over 50 agreed to take redundancy.

"We agreed to abandon the South Pit which had geological problems but we still had two very good seams of top qualify coking coal to exploit.

"We also drew up a case that we should be allowed to tap into the reserves which the proposed Margam superpit was due to mine.

"We demonstrated that these reserves were accessible to our mine at far less than the cost of sinking a new pit."

The miners then arranged their own independent public inquiry in Cardiff where expert witnesses were called to back their case.

The result of the inquiry, conducted by four eminent men from outside of the industry, was in favour of keeping the pit open and the full report was sent to the NCB's main board in London when it reviewed the pit's position. But to no avail.

"They decided to go ahead with closure despite all our arguments," said Mr Isaac.

Appeal

The men still had one option left – to appeal against closure.

"But in November, a mass meeting of 500 men voted by just 30 to give up the fight.

The pit closed within weeks and men either took redundancy or transferred to other mines.

"Had there been a chance of buying St John's and running it ourselves like Tower, we would have gone for it," he said.

Ironically, the NCB's pledge that it would tap the vast Margam reserves with a new mine – denounced as a sham at the time by the miners – has never been fulfilled although Celtic Energy has now put forward a much smaller scheme which also entails opencast mining.

"What has happened is a tragedy," said Mr Isaac.

"There are still vast reserves of coal that could be economically mined in this area.

"We have seen the decimation of a proud industry for the sake of political dogma.

"There were 23 deep mines in South Wales when the strike started and now we have only one – Tower."

The Garw Colliery employed more than 600 men when the decision to close it was taken in the autumn of 1985.

The men called in experts to put together a rescue package for the mine which would have been exactly 100 years old in January 1986 – the month that it closed.

The pit had a proud history and in the 1970s, the men smashed productivity records in South Wales by producing 64cwt per manshift.

But after the return to work following the strike, the men were given new production targets which meant an increase from 4,000 tonnes a week to 7,000 tonnes – a task described at the time by lodge secretary Berwyn Howells as "Mission Impossible."

In December 1985, the men gathered at the pit for the last time, hauled down the NCB flag and set it on fire.

"We had such high hopes of the industry when the NCB was set up," said former miner Will Trigg at the time.

"We were proud of that flag. Now, people regard the coal board as the enemy of the miners and our communities."

And the area's third mine – Wyndham-Western in the Ogmore Valley – also closed after the strike although the decision to shut it was taken before the strike started.

The men here also fought hard to keep it open but to no avail.

A Note to Arthur Scargill

Arthur Scargill for President Election Campaign.

A Note to Arthur Scargill
November 1987

ELECTION CAMPAIGN
ARTHUR SCARGILL FOR PRESIDENT
A SCHEDULE

WALES

(1)   In line with our discussion I have arranged for a mass meeting probably in the Pontyberem Welfare Hall (near the Cynheidre Colliery) for Monday evening 14th Dec. The Lodge will also possibly ask you to visit the New Carway Fawr development adjacent to the pit at five roads near Llanelli. This will be a good opportunity to be seen with rank and File miners in working clothes at a Pit environment.

(2)   I have arranged for the Tower Lodge to have a mass meeting that will take in the Rhondda and Aberdare area some time in January (you will need to give me a date for this. In addition moves will be made in Tower, Cynhiedre, Blaenant, Bettws, Penallta, Six Bells and Trelewis Drift to call on the Area Conference to nominate Arthur Scargill. The possiblity exists that S. Wales will either end up nominating no-one or Arthur Scargill. I have discussed with Lodge Leaders and rank and File men in all these Pits how to approach this matter in the course of the next two weeks.

(3)   A Venue in Abertillary in the East of the Coalfield can be arranged and I would need an open date for this.

Scotland. Joe Owens Chairman of Bilston Glen has offered to arrange a mass meeting in Edinburgh Area. A date for this would be helpful. I know that you are in Seafield on the 14th Dec. The Scebta delegate John Shaw will be of assistance in this matter.

Durham. I have been in contact with Stan Pearce, delegate Monkwearmouth for meetings in that Area. And he will discuss with me the details of any campaign.

Western area. Steve Sullivan, Delegate Sutton Manor will place himself at the disposal of the campaign in the Lankashire Coalfield and the North Wales Pit.

Derbyshire. John Dunn of Markham Colliery is available in this difficult Coalfield to discuss tactics and organise meetings etc.

Northumberland. Kevin Maughn Area Chairman and John Cunningham Executive member is in touch with me and metings can be arranged there. One may be sufficent in Ashington.

Midlands. I am in touch with rank and File miners in Littleton Colliery who are keen to help.

Kent. You will have your own contacts there. I also am in touch with rank and File miners there and I am also a Friend from long ago of Malcom Pitt.

Yorkshire. Your campaign here is more than likely sorted out. But additional support will be organise by Richard Clarkson in the North and Gary Ironmonger in the South.

I propose that we have further meeting towards the end of this week to go over fine detail that whole tenure of the campaign if this meets with your approval.

Ian Isaac. S. Wales Area.

Pages from the Mineworker

THE **Mineworker**

Journal of the National Miners' Broad Left   5p

FIGHT NOW

FLEXIBLE WORKING

DISCIPLINARY CODE

BUILD A

FIGHTING

UNION

HUNDREDS OF individual rank and file miners who support the National Miners' Broad Left have worked in every area of the British coalfield for the return of Arthur Scargill as the only candidate prepared to fight for unity around the policies as agreed at successive national conferences of our union. The presidential campaign has dealt with the issues that confront miners in the pits, workshops and units.

SIX DAY WORKING

On six day working, Scargill has consistently explained that this would mean the closure of at least 32 more pits if implemented widely throughout the British mining industry. The ploy in South Wales to blackmail miners into accepting the 'concept of six day production' by the Coal Board has been opposed by the rank and file.

This election has been the first opportunity that Welsh miners and others will have had to express their views and their resistance to the Americanisation of our industry.

British coal have attempted to create the climate of a six day production by pushing 'flexible working' through the back door at certain pits under the guise of increasing production to save the pit or meet production targets. As predicted by the National Miners' Broad Left, the Board have put the proposed new link mine at Thorne in Yorkshire into moth balls as blackmail tactics over six day production in the same manner as they have done over the Margam project in Wales, and at Frances/Seafield in Scotland.

Miners have a genuine desire for new pits to open and to protect our industry. They will provide the effort and skill necessary to work these; but on conditions and representation historically fought for by rank and file miners and socialist leaders over the years.

BREAKAWAY OUTFIT

The deliberate interference by the UDM, offering to press-gang miners into their breakaway outfit at new mines is reminiscent of union busting activities in America of the 1930's. They claim that they represent the best interests of miners in wages and conditions yet, in a recent table of area average earnings published by British Coal, Notts were sixth in the league behind the vast majority of NUM members.

Talk of a merger with the UDM is alien to the needs and desires of rank and file miners.

But, union-busting can take many forms—such as the vicious disciplinary code.   **Continued on back page**

AROUND THE COALFIELDS   Miners fight back!

Bentley miners lobby South Yorkshire panel meeting.

No to management intimidation

Bentley miners walked out on strike immediately after the Christmas holidays.Three men found themselves replaced by the management and transferred to other tasks, just as their drivage was about to enter a position where possibly large bonus could be earned.

By the Thursday, the South Yorkshire coalfield was virtually completely picketed out. On the Friday the dispute began to spread into North Yorkshire with Kellingley and pits in the Selby complex joining the dispute.

By now, management were making threatening noises about using an injunction against the strike. Had they attempted to use the courts, they would only have provoked an even angrier response from the miners.

It appears that management at Bentley have backed down to an extent in face of the struggle. They offered the NUM at the pit a disputes procedure and have also agreed not to put new men into the drivage in the meantime.

OVER THE last few weeks, 2000 Welsh miners, 20 per cent of the coalfield, have shown their willingness to fight British Coal's bully boy tactics and the introduction of flexible working.

In Marine colliery, Ebbw Vale, strike action was taken to defend union activist David Edwards. He was sacked for gross misconduct, over an unproven hoax fire call. British Coal then threatened all the men with the sack if they took further action to defend comrade Edwards.

In Deep Navigation colliery, Treharris, 750 men struck against new underground manning levels. The men only returned to work, while talks proceeded, after threats by management that unless the stoppage was ended, the future of the pit would be jeopardised.

Men in Taff-Merthyr mine, near Bedlinog, struck for over two weeks. Taff-Merthyr is one of the most profitable pits in the coalfield, yet even here management attempted to turn the screw. British Coal proposed a change from 3 to 4 shift working, to carry out vital repairs on a roadway. The real reason was summed up by the lodge secretary, "The Board are attempting to introduce 6-day working through the back-door". The men have given their answer.

It is unfortunate that the South Wales executive are out of touch with the feeling of their members. George Rees should listen to the men rather than advocate flexible working.

Bilston Glen colliery in Scotland struck before Christmas, returning to work to impose a FULL overtime ban. The men were protesting at management attempts to impose new shift arrangements—'flexible working' by the back-door?

T H E **Mineworker**
Journal of the National Miners' Broad Left

SPECIAL ISSUE

CODE OF CONDUCT

THE MINERS at Frickley and Stillingfleet can testify how British Coal's unilateral code could be used to isolate or even sack union activists. Branch committees would be prevented from representing the day to day problems of the men by the fear of suspension or discipline under this draconian code. We must fight as miners under the national union to get a fair code which would allow the principle of nominated representation and fairness.

PIT CLOSURES

Pits have been closed because they have been isolated in their fight. Only a campaign involving the communities, other trade unions in the energy sector, and a firm lead from area and national leaders will stand a chance of saving pits.

Miners at Darfield Main fought and won such a battle under the Tory climate of economic competition and pegging low prices of coal to the CEGB.

After recovering from the financial hardships of the 84/85 strike, after a period of reflection, miners throughout the British coalfield have shown their willingness to fight back. More walkouts and strikes over discipline, flexible working and management intransigence have occurred in mining than in any other industry. What is now needed is a united union to fight back, improving its democratic structures to reflect the views and problems of the rank and file. This can only be provided by a campaigning socialist leadership in the NUM. So when will the 'new realists' stand for re-election?

PRIVATISATION

It was reported in the *Independent* in December that the world price of steam c_ _ is due to rise from $30 per tonne to $45 per tonne by the middle of 1989. And further, up to $60 per tonne by the early 1990s for a combination of reasons involving the costs of multi-national oil companies in America and the economic strain of coal subsidies in Australia and elsewhere. If this happened, pits would become, in British Coal's criteria, 'economic overnight' in the same way that they became 'uneconomic overnight' in the 1970's. There is no need for our industry to be butchered to a 30 super pit industry under privatisation with massive sterilisation of coal reserves in every coalfield.

A campaign by miners AND other energy workers against privatisation would lead to the saving of pits and power stations and prevent the suicidal march towards nuclear power generation. The National Miners' Broad Left calls on Arthur Scargill, on the basis of his renewed mandate, to lead that campaign. The BLOC conference of 13 February could be just the place to start it.

BROAD LEFT ORGANISING COMMITTEE

Conference '88
Sheffield City Hall, Sat 13 February
Speakers include Tony Benn

IT HAS never been more important for trade union activists to get together and organise. At a time of unprecedented attacks from the Tories—new trade union legislation, more plans to sell off nationalised industries, attacks on education and housing, their attempts to emasculate Labour local authorities—there is a real need for the strength of the movement to be harnessed in opposition.

Unfortunately, the vast bulk of the TUC and national union leadership have been notable by their silence. 'New realism', it seems, is the order of the day. Such a policy is more akin to Nero fiddling while Rome burns.

Activists from across the trade union movement who are prepared to fight will gather in Sheffield on 13 February to hammer out a policy and strategy to turn the tide against the Tories. Make sure your union branch or workplace is represented!

All trade union bodies (branches, workplaces, district committees, divisional councils etc) can send up to five delegates. The fee per delegate is £3. For application form and details of local transport to the conference, write to Broad Left Organising Committee, PO box 464, London E5 8PT. All cheques should be made payable to BLOC.

JOIN THE BROAD LEFT

I would like to find out more about the Miners' Broad Left .... ☐
I would like to be notified of future events/conferences .... ☐
I hereby enclose a donation of £............
(Cheques: 'National Miners' Broad Left)
Please sent me........copies of *The Mineworker* at a cost of 5p each (cash with order)
Name ....
Address....................................
....
Lodge/Branch/Area ....
....
Tel no ....
Return to: 'National Miners' Broad Left, c/o 39 Gold Street, Barnsley, South Yorkshire.

Published by National Miners' Broad Left, 39 Gold Street, Barnsley, South Yorkshire. Printed by Eastway Offset, 3/13 Hepscott Road, London E9